JACK OUT OF THE BOX:

A Practical Guide to the Open Classroom

by LEE L. SMITH

For those teachers who are challenged by the difficult task of meeting each student's learning needs, here is a complete, practical guide that provides a clear, in-depth explanation of the open classroom technique.

Accompanied by dozens of restructuring methods ready for easy implementation, this exceptional volume covers every aspect of the nongraded approach to individualized instruction.

Here are the most productive techniques and methods ever developed for creating open classrooms, with the emphasis on sharing ideas, experiences and activities that have been used successfully by the nation's leading educators. m

Sample bulletins for teachers, organizational charts, sample letters, individual student schedule plans, record forms, modular schedules, floor plans, schedules of special teachers, and community survey forms are presented in a practical, easy-to-understand format.

In addition, photographs of workable open classroom set-ups provide the necessary illustrations for developing a successful program in any educational environment with the least amount of effort.

EVERYTHING YOU NEED TO INDIVIDUALIZE INSTRUCTION

Dr. Lee L. Smith, a noted educator in the field of open classroom planning, has spent years developing his modern methods. Now he has put his immense know-how into this comprehensive volume. You'll discover:

- **How to use flexible grouping through the use of specific instructional materials**
- **How to develop a flexible concept of school organization**
- **How to use team teaching, nongrading and learning centers to create open classrooms**
- **How to keep records of individual progress**
- **How to improve communication and staff morale**
- **How to involve the total community in the open classroom educational enterprise**

What's more, this book includes administrative bulletins for making specific suggestions to teachers, ideas for in-service training, and sug-

JACK
OUT
OF
THE
BOX

A PRACTICAL GUIDE
TO THE OPEN CLASSROOM

Lee L. Smith

Parker Publishing Company, Inc.
West Nyack, N.Y.

JACK OUT OF THE BOX
A PRACTICAL GUIDE TO THE OPEN CLASSROOM
by Lee L. Smith

©1974, by

Parker Publishing Company, Inc.
West Nyack, N.Y.

Library of Congress Cataloging in Publication Data

Smith, Lee L
    Jack out of the box.

    1. Open plan schools. I. Title.
LB1029.06S6   372.1'3   73-12685
ISBN 0-13-509182-9

Printed in the United States of America

OTHER BOOKS BY THE AUTHOR

*A Practical Approach to the
Nongraded Elementary School*

Teaching in a Nongraded School

This Book Is Dedicated to

the Staff and Community

of

Longfellow Elementary School

How This Book Will Help You
Establish Open Classrooms

A song, "Little Boxes," written by Malvina Reynolds,[1] illustrates how living has become a process of conforming. The words to the song follow:

Little boxes on the hillside...Little boxes made of ticky-tacky,
Little boxes on the hillside...Little boxes all the same.
There's a green one and a pink one and a blue one and a yellow one,
And they're all made out of ticky-tacky and they all look just the same.

And the people in the houses, all went to the university
Where they were put in boxes and they came out all the same.
And there's doctors, and there's lawyers, and business executives
And they're all made out of ticky-tacky and they all look just the same.

And they all play on the golf course, and drink their martinis dry,
And they all have pretty children and the children go to school
And the children go to summer camp, and then to the university,
Where they are put in boxes, and they come out all the same.

And the boys go into business and marry and raise a family,
And they all get put in boxes, little boxes all the same.
There's a green one and a pink one and a blue one and a yellow one.
And they're all made out of ticky-tacky and they all look just the same.

---

[1] Words and music by Malvina Reynolds Copyright 1962 by Schroder Music Co. (ASCAP). Used by permission.

ACKNOWLEDGMENTS

Mr. Jamie Hess for assistance with photography.

Mr. Paul Churchill for suggestions and illustrations.

Personal friends for their expressed confidence and support.

The family for encouragement.

And so it is with education: Jack is in a box. Traditional classroom structure is based on the assumption that children learn passively from what the teacher "tells" them. Often children are told to sit down and to keep quiet because they come to school to "learn." Children soon regulate themselves to the system, that is, they conform.

This same traditional attitude has been carried into adult life: some teachers are afraid to try anything new or different because their security would be threatened; principals often become satisfied with maintaining the "status quo" so as to keep their positions; supervisors and superintendents do not want to "rock the boat" because of parent and community reactions; parents and other laymen resist change because they have not been involved in planning for it and feel secure in that which they know and understand. Whether he be child or adult, Jack is boxed in by conformity.

Familiar Quotations

WHAT'S WRONG WITH A GRADED CURRICULUM? IT WAS GOOD ENOUGH FOR ME....

I MEAN, WE'VE ALWAYS DONE IT THIS WAY....

IT CAN'T BE DONE, IT'LL NEVER WORK...

BUT WHAT ABOUT THE STANDARDS?

ISN'T THIS JUST ANOTHER TRICK BY RADICALS?

WELL, WHEN I WAS A BOY...

ETC, ETC, ETC.......

Innovators are aware that traditional classroom structure is not supportive of the ways in which people learn. Many attempts have been made in recent years to get Jack out of his box. The literature abounds with terms such as: individualized instruction; relevant curriculum; humanistic education; non-gradedness; team teaching; flexible scheduling; the integrated day; continuous progress; British Primary; free schools; self-pacing; open space; programmed instruction; I.P.I.; modular scheduling; planned communities; informal education; creative teaching and learning; open university; learning centers; schools without walls; etc.

The scope of this book stems from the conviction that education is not a problem to be solved, but rather a life to be lived. The open classroom, which is based on this approach, can become a reality by combining the best from these innovations with the best from tradition.

It is difficult to define an open classroom in a brief, specific statement. This book will provide the reader with the basic tenets of the open classroom philosophy and describe specific ways in which classrooms may become "open."

I will include ideas, experiences, and activities that have been used successfully in developing a practical approach toward the open classroom in old, traditional buildings as well as in modern new facilities.

An open classroom is a "doing" place. It provides a smorgasbord of activities and opportunities for students. The curriculum includes arranging school facilities, providing materials, and managing social relationships and activities to promote worthwhile and productive living for individuals.

Since nongrading is concerned with meeting individual needs, it has become a vehicle for creating open classrooms. Team teaching enhances the development of the idea that most human learning is the result of interrelationships of human beings as they develop in social situations. This book shows how the organizational patterns of nongradedness and team teaching can be used to establish open classrooms.

Included is a discussion of the concept of learning centers as an organizational format for arranging instructional activities. This will provide greater opportunities for individualized teaching and facilitate independent learning in open classrooms.

This book is for those who want their involvement in the educational enterprise to make a difference in the lives of boys and girls and men and women—for those who want to help get JACK OUT OF THE BOX.

—LEE L. SMITH

ABOUT THE AUTHOR

LEE L. SMITH, Ed.D., was the principal of the Brunswick Elementary School, Brunswick, Maryland. He developed a successful and widely-acclaimed nongraded, team teaching program there, and the school was selected by the National Education Association as a demonstration center for the Year-of-the-Non-Conference. Dr. Smith is currently the principal of Longfellow Elementary School in Columbia, Maryland and Director of the Teaching for Living Institute, which offers national seminars on open education. Formerly Assistant to the Dean of Education at George Washington University, Dr. Smith has lectured extensively to professional groups, schools and school systems, civic and parent groups and college classes about open education. His previously published works include A PRACTICAL APPROACH TO THE NONGRADED ELEMENTARY SCHOOL and TEACHING IN A NONGRADED SCHOOL.

0-13-509182-

Table of Contents

chapter one | The Objectives of the Open Classroom

Education was originally conceived as a means of handing down to youth the "way of life" in their culture. Before there were any formal schools, children learned by participating in carrying on activities: Girls aided mothers with domestic chores to learn how to help; boys watched men and learned how to hunt and fish. Introduction to ceremony—perhaps the first formal school —became the method of passing on to youth the selected aspects of tribal culture.

In the earliest stages of schooling, there were two dimensions to education: on the one hand, children were taught in formal situations at specific times and places the facts deemed important by the elders; on the other hand, children learned through living the group life such things as domestic duties, moral and social attitudes, the language of daily life and means of livelihood.

Through the years, the school has become the place where children are expected to master subject matter as preparation for adult life. Unfortunately, this education at "school" has been separated from the processes of life, as if one *learns* only in school and *lives* only outside of school. This institutionalized approach has concentrated on teaching curricula rather than human beings. Teachers have become dispensers of information in order to cover the designated material; students have been expected to listen, review and memorize; all students have been required to complete the same books and to master the same content: Each has learned to conform.

THE PHILOSOPHY OF THE OPEN CLASSROOM

The basic tenet of the philosophy of the open classroom is that education is a "live-in." Every child has the potential for many types of growth. Some lie dormant throughout life; others are developed in part. The determination of which possibilities are realized and the degree to which any is fulfilled is a function of the environment.

If children are to develop their intellectual potential, the school must provide an environment that is intellectually stimulating and in which achievement of an intellectual nature is respected and nurtured. The emotional climate of a learning situation determines how well the pupil will obtain functional behavioral changes. Unless the emotional content of the situation is conducive to the acceptance of new information, that information will appear irrelevant and will be rejected. In every situation, boys and girls and men and women are striving to feel right about themselves, to feel that they have worth, to feel that they are accepted.

Each person is uniquely different. Meeting individual differences is not a technique; it is a way of living—a style of life. It includes accepting others, respecting their contributions, working for the kind of group operation in which each individual knows he has a part, and encouraging each to give his best in each situation.

Although it is quite important to learn to live with other people, it is imperative that each person learn to live with himself. Each must learn to understand his assets and use them constructively. He must discover his shortcomings and, if possible, improve them. He must develop a sense of responsibility to others and a balancing sense of self-protection sufficient to keep him functioning at an efficient level. Complete understanding of oneself is a continuous process. Successful living is not a thing but a process, a continuous movement toward ever-changing value goals.

The primary function of the open classroom is to provide an environment that will enhance the development of values and attitudes. The curriculum should not be a formal one emphasizing mastery of subject matter as an end in itself; rather, it should emphasize the development of the child and take into consideration his interests, abilities and experiences. The subject matter should be presented in such a way as to help him grasp its functional value in relation to the problems of everyday living with which he is confronted.

All learning should deal with aspects of the society in which the child lives and the ways in which these aspects are important to him. The child's experience should be related directly to his environment and thus enable him to acquire the tools he will need as he continues to grow.

Teachers must provide many opportunities for a growing, responsible independence, with each child gradually accepting more responsibility for his own learning and assuming greater self-direction. Emphasis should be placed on the personal development of the individual and on self-understanding.

A child's development of a positive self-concept, of attitudes and values and of standards of behavior is influenced by the atmosphere and the environment in which he lives and learns. A well-developed human being is one who has self-respect, because this is a basic need in all humans. A major task of the teacher is to help each child develop and maintain self-respect.

The activities of a child are directed toward satisfying his needs. His growth pattern affects his behavior and he has problems when he cannot satisfy his needs. All of his behavior is *caused.* In order to help each child find satisfaction in learning and to develop self-confidence, the school should plan a program to help children live a better and richer life both in and out of school.

Children look to teachers for guidance in the solution of their everyday problems; they expect teachers to be able to understand and help solve the problems of group living. Children also look to the teacher as the expert in human relations. The teacher should guide children in making decisions that will result in higher qualities of living and provide experiences that will lead to higher levels of thinking.

The teacher should see her role as a resource person; she should provide guidance in group activities of planning, fulfilling and evaluating the total program; she should help children interpret the values and attitudes developed through living together in the open classroom.

THE HUMAN ELEMENT

In this century we have learned a great deal about people. We know that the human personality is built by the individual's response to life and particularly to other people. Teaching is the art of arranging conditions to challenge responses that aid in the development of rich, warm, sensitive human beings.

Figure 1-1

All human behavior is social; it involves other people. Traditionally, the school has not permitted children to cooperate or to help each other with any school work. Direct communication among pupils has not been allowed.

A child comes to school and we say to him, "Sit down and keep quiet. You came here to learn and we're going to teach you." Once again, we imply that he lives outside school and learns inside school, as if living and learning were separate. The philosophy of the school should be that we learn as we work and live together in school and out of school.

The art of teaching is demonstrated in arranging conditions and circumstances that provide experiences productive of better human behavior. Goals must be genuine and appropriate to the learner. These are the criteria for evaluating the experiences of children. Nothing good can be built into a personality by coercion, because all human activity is directed to the attainment of its own goals.

The quality of the child's living affects the quality of his personal development. The day-to-day living of a child is built into his physical organism. The quality of his experience is the crucial factor in determining the quality of his developing personality, and schools must provide these kinds of experiences. We cannot teach our children in an atmosphere of strict control and expect them to learn to live as freedom-loving children.

Human Interaction

Most human learning is not the result of instruction; rather it is the result of interrelationships of human beings as they develop in social situations. Educators must arrange school facilities, provide materials, manage social relationships and activities that will promote worthwhile and productive living for children. Our profession must evaluate its efforts in terms of human behavior; we must evaluate in terms of the quality of living of every child.

The more one looks at the pupils as participants in a social system the more clearly a message comes through: Although the school may treat pupils as members of groups, the learning that takes place is individual. However, an analysis of many school systems indicates that the emphasis has remained in instruction (what is done for pupils) rather than learning (what pupils actually do).

Every effort should be made by educational leaders to bring about changes that may be needed to provide the kind of educational program that will enable students to attain self-fulfillment. The school should endeavor to have the kind of educational experience available for each student that will best meet his needs. We need to view students as persons who are enacting roles in a school situation; we need to provide the kind of educational program that brings the school's expectations of student roles and the student's own expectations into close harmony. We need to use the students' own values for continuing guidance in decision-making; this will lead both pupils and teachers toward more meaningful relationships with each other. The emphasis should be upon learning by the pupils, with student self-control the number-one goal.

The most important characteristic of the school is the human element. It is important for the teacher to see each child as a unique human being, neither good nor bad except as his living makes him that way. The teacher must see each child as having purposes of his own and a pattern of growth that he must follow in order to develop *his* feelings and *his* attitudes, because *his* living demands this.

PURPOSES AND GOALS OF THE OPEN CLASSROOM

The purposes of the open classroom should be:

- to create a relaxed atmosphere that will free teachers and students from unnecessary pressures and allow them to develop their creative potential.
- to adjust the teaching and administrative procedures to meet differing social, mental and physical capacities.
- to establish for each a pattern of success.

- to provide opportunities for each to learn according to his own growth pattern and style.
- to encourage diversity and creativity.
- to provide an environment that will enhance the development of attitudes and values.
- to provide many opportunities for a growing, responsible independence.

With these basic purposes in mind, the specific goals of the open classroom should be:

- to help each find satisfaction in learning.
- to help each realize that subject-matter skills are tools he should use in meeting and solving problems.
- to help each develop self-confidence.
- to help each think imaginatively and openly explore his ideas.
- to help each free himself to explore the resources of the school and community (both human and material) as well as his own resources.
- to help each assume responsibility for his own learning.
- to help each to become self-directed and self-disciplined.

These purposes and goals can be fulfilled by creating an open classroom atmosphere that promotes the philosophy that school is an extension of everyone's style of living. Education becomes a life to be lived rather than a problem to be solved.

chapter two | The Curriculum and the Open Classroom

In open classrooms the curriculum can be defined as *that which happens to pupils;* it includes all of the experiences that are made available to them. Curriculum is not synonomous with "course of study"; it is not just a listing of subject matter to be covered by teachers. It includes interpersonal relationships as well.

Those of us who advocate open classrooms feel strongly that most human learning is not the result of instruction, but that it is the result of interrelationships among human beings as they develop in social situations. Hence, the curriculum for open classrooms includes arranging school facilities, providing materials and managing social relationships and activities to promote worthwhile and productive living for children.

INDIVIDUALIZED LEARNING

Almost every child comes to school as a curious and energetic human being. In an open classroom this little bundle of energy should have many activities and experiences to keep him "turned on."

Each pupil needs to feel important and that his questions are welcomed. He needs to know that the purposes of the open classroom are to meet his needs and concerns, to help him overcome his fears and anxieties and to satisfy his curiosities. We must be sincerely concerned about the welfare of each child and accept him for what he is. We can provide flexible grouping, one-to-one situations or independent study and call this individualized instruction—but what we should really be concerned about is *individualized learning*. Regardless of the teaching alternatives we provide, the learning that takes place is by each individual.

The social development of an individual is a process of interrelated transactions between the organism and its environment. Development is modifiable throughout life rather than being set and unalterable on the basis of early life experiences only. The child modifies his behavior so that there are changes in specific behavior appropriate to internal changes and external demands. The social context provides patterns of information that serve as stimuli, to which the growing body must respond. The results are called patterns of behavior. From these patterns come emotion, values, attitudes and self-concepts.

Adequate socialization is the most important single accomplishment of a human being, for man's most significant learning and development take place in the context of social interaction with other human beings. There is a great distance between the state in which the child finds himself as he leaves the family and the one toward which he must strive. After the family, the school is the first social institution that an individual must deal with. It is the place in which he first learns to handle himself with strangers.

The primary function of the school program should be to provide an environment that will enhance the development of values and attitudes. The social understandings, skills and attitudes that the child acquires will enable him to make a satisfactory transition from the society of the home to that of the school.

Well-planned programs should include content, activities, and materials pertaining to human relationships in the home, school, community, and other places. Experiences should be provided to help children become effective as individuals and as group members. Every subject in the curriculum should lead each pupil to find himself as an integral part of a continuous sphere of humanity. We should be as familiar as possible with our neighbors of the world in order to prepare children for the land of tomorrow. We must concentrate on human values and social sciences—the curriculum must be internationally minded.

Teachers must spend more time in helping each student understand the political and social problems of the world. The student should be made aware that man is still evolving and that he has a share in making the great expectations of the human race come true.

Children need to become skillful in human relations, economically efficient and accepting of certain civic responsibilities. In order for these values to be *really* learned by children they must be *lived* in all phases of the school program. Therefore, all learning should deal with aspects of the society in which the child lives and ways in which these aspects are important to him. The purpose of these learning activities is to enable the child to acquire and develop skills, understandings and attitudes that will help him live effectively and happily in his environment. Successful living is not a thing but a process, a continuous movement toward ever-changing value goals.

The child's social environment expands markedly during the middle-childhood years. In the continuing interaction between the developing child and his expanding environment, some motives become strengthened and more clearly articulated while others diminish in importance; new standards are set; he is confronted with new problems and challenges.

The school becomes the center of the child's extrafamilial life. The kinds of teachers he has, the teaching methods he encounters and the types of materials to which he is exposed will have important effects upon his general capacity to meet and master new challenges and to develop self-confidence and self-esteem.

GENERAL PRINCIPLES OF SOCIAL DEVELOPMENT

In his book, *Child Development: The Emerging Self,* Don C. Dinkmeyer[1] presents an excellent description of the principles of social development and the implications of these for teachers to consider as they work with children. Dr. Dinkmeyer says:

> The child learns methods of appropriate social interactions in the family, with his peers, and from significant others. The quality and quantity of these contacts should stimulate social development. The child can learn social behavior only by participating in the give and take of interpersonal relations.

> Responsible adults need to be as aware of this area as of mental development.

> Children are taught to manage their needs in line with specific cultural expectations. The teacher must be aware of the cultural and subculture expectations of each child in order to understand behavior adequately. The school can assist children in understanding variances in cultural expectations.

> Dependency upon mother is a prerequisite for the development of the child's independence. Mother must realize that it is an important developmental step to have the child become dependent upon her for acceptance and approval.

> Acceptance and forcing are important concepts as the child moves from dependence to independence. The parent must be willing to permit the child increasing participation in decision making and avoid pushing him to take on only those responsibilities the parent wants to give up.

> Dependency is a consistent trait in females from childhood to adulthood. This trait in the member of the family primarily responsible for child training has implications for the type of security the young child experiences. The girl child is rewarded for dependent

---

[1]Don C. Dinkmeyer, *Child Development: The Emerging Self,* © 1965, pp. 176-178. Reprinted by permission of Prentice-Hall, Inc., Englewood Cliffs, N.J.

behavior, which is less acceptable in the boy and may influence his self-acceptance.

Dependency fails to develop without experiencing consistent gratification from some person. The early management of children has long-range effects.

Physical punishment tends to produce aggressive children. Parents who provide frequent physical punishment would appear to be engaging in a self-perpetuating series of interactions.

The specific traits valued by the society and the subculture influence development of the child's traits. Society's institutions must deal realistically with these varying value systems.

Some children come to school educationally disadvantaged owing to membership in certain social classes. Educational planning by the teacher must recognize these differences and attempt to provide appropriate experiences.

The learning of human relationships occurs first in the family setting. More education in understanding these relationships should be provided for future parents while they are in school. The school frequently requires an understanding of everything but self, and self in relationship to others. This educational experience could be of great value in a preventive sense.

Democratic living practiced in the home has been shown to enable the child to participate more effectively in the school experience. The home should provide the opportunity to operate in an atmosphere that permits choice and accepting the responsibility for one's choice.

The peer group affords the child contact with varied religious, socioeconomic, and ethnic backgrounds in a setting devoid of authoritarian relationships. Peers make concrete some of the lessons alluded to within the family setting. Due to the significance of peer relationships, the teacher must take them into account in planning learning experiences.

The expectancies of the family and family constellation should be similar to the peer group's and significant others' if socialization is to take place rapidly. When there is great divergency between these forces—when the family, for example, values certain customs and rituals which are ridiculed by the other groups—the child may tend to fluctuate his values in line with the social setting of the moment.

Children vary in their readiness for social contacts, their need for social contacts, and in the rate that they enter or leave some relationships. Adult acceptance of the child's attitudes instead of forcing promotes social development.

Entrance to school demands increased social contacts from the child. Organization of the learning experience so that it facilitates these contacts is a responsibility of educators.

The discipline of the group is frequently more effective than discipline by adults. Educators must observe the discipline of the group, permit it to function when wholesome, and provide guidance when it is detrimental to the objectives of education.

The skills necessary for forming adequate friendships are teachable. While these skills might be best acquired in the family at an early age, guidance activities in the classroom, discussion groups, and in some instances individual counseling can serve to provide reorientation in this area.

Social maturity is evidenced in the capacity of the child to maintain friendships that meet the needs of others as well as his own. This type of activity by the child should be encouraged.

Successful goal attainment often produces renewed and increased striving for the goal. It is important to provide goals which, while adequate in their challenge, also provide opportunities for success.

The motivation for achievement in boys and girls is significantly different. Girls may be motivated by teacher approval, but boys are more likely to be motivated by activities that permit self approval.

A continual series of negative commands serves as a deterrent to the child's courage and social development. It is important to seek adequate elements of the child's functioning and encourage these. Focus on the child's unacceptable behavior may only guarantee the establishment of such behavior.

It is important to avoid giving a social reward to "bad behavior." The adult's concern and involvement in the elimination of a trait frequently provide the reward that sustains the trait.

Children become responsible as we provide opportunities for assuming responsibility. If responsible behavior is a prerequisite for assuming responsibility, many children can never develop in this area. Responsibilities are frequently given to children who need them least.

Attitudes related to racial and religious groups are learned early in childhood, and are a reflection of parental values and the subculture. Attitude formation must be an early school concern if changes are expected.

The social climate of the group has a significant effect on the attitudes developed by members of the group. The teacher who wants to develop self- and group-sustained activities organizes the class on a democratic basis.

Group discussion is effective in promoting social development. It must give the child a genuine chance to participate and to express himself. While this discussion can occur on an impromptu basis, there should be regular planned periods for group discussion.

Sociometric evaluations should lead to action on the part of the teacher. Seating arrangements and committee work should foster development. Some children can develop most adequately by being permitted to encourage the socially discouraged.

Social behavior tends to become constant and persist. We are cautioned against assuming that social traits are all related to stages that will pass.

STRUCTURED VS. UNSTRUCTURED CURRICULUM

The open classroom should be child-centered and should recognize the importance of the interest of the learner and his involvement in planning his own activities. Traditional classroom structure is not supportive of ways in which children learn because it is based on the assumption that children learn passively what the teacher tells them.

We need a vastly enriched environment that allows children

to explore with concrete materials and to interact with others. (See Figure 2-1). Children learn best when they are following their own interests or questioning their own experiences.

Figure 2-1

I think the most critical issue is that of the extent to which the school should influence the development of the child. There are those who advocate complete freedom for the child. At the other extreme are those who advocate complete molding of the learner through imposition of a fixed and final curriculum. The choice should not be limited to either of these two extremes. I strongly believe that neither is possible or feasible. Rather, we should incorporate the best of each extreme into a practical and realistic approach to curriculum planning.

Too many educators rave jumped on the bandwagon of "freedom" in schools without fully understanding the meaning of this approach. They have become so committed to "motion" that they fail to establish purposes. They become satisfied merely with movement—even with movement in circles.

Children must be taught to set purposes and to use their

freedom wisely in achieving their goals and objectives. Just as the educator should know what he is doing and accept full responsibility for his acts, so should the child. Without some guidance from adults, a child may enjoy a certain kind of freedom, but not the kind he really wants. He doesn't really want to waste his time and move around the school without a purpose or a plan; he really wants some direction.

Freedom is the power of effective choice; choice demands viable alternatives. Freedom is a mental attitude; it is not an end in itself, but a means by which thinking, judging, evaluating and acting may be integrated into the development of individual capacity. In the open classroom freedom should be *for* instruction, not *from* instruction. This new freedom is toward self-direction and self-discipline. Emphasis must be on learning (what pupils actually do) rather than instruction (what is done for pupils).

Figure 2-2

Flexibility in Grouping

In speaking of this topic, Dr. B. Frank Brown[2] says

When the educational process is loosened, learning is approached in violently different ways. Subject matter for some consists of studying the basic skills. For others, subject matter is almost entirely problem solving. The object of Appropriate Placement is to provide a curriculum with differing variations. The intent of the curriculum in this school is to jar students by the unexpected: to force them to an unusual or creative response by a condition of uncertainty. The purpose is to activate curiosity, which is excited when a reasonable amount of uncertainty is introduced into a learning situation. If too little uncertainty is initiated, students become bored; when too much is brought in they become frustrated. The skillful teacher knows just how much uncertainty to bring into the learning situation.

The progress of education can only be in the direction of the Appropriate Placement School, for there is simply no other direction to take. The entire purpose of Appropriate Placement is to educate for flexibility. The placement process is designed to give students flexibility of attitude and mind. In an era of unparalleled break-throughs in science and computer technology, individuals must have a 'built in' kind of expertise with which they can quickly acquire new skills when old skills are automated away. Present trends indicate that the average individual will need to be re-trained three times as a result of the inroads of automation. This calls for a ground swell in the direction of flexible education.

In education by evolution, much has been written and said about scholastic excellence. In revolutionized education much is being written about curiosity and imagination, as types of excellence, but unfortunately these are types which graded schools have indeed neglected. Schools have always recognized, nourished, and applauded academic excellence, but there has been no reward or recognition for curiosity, an ability which might lead students to learn what they are not expected to know. Faced with the enormous problem of educating boys and girls for professions which do not yet exist and

---

[2] B. Frank Brown, *The Appropriate Placement School: A Sophisticated Non-graded Curriculum*, © 1965 by Parker Publishing Company, Inc., West Nyack, N.Y.

t now be described, education must be revolutionized at least
e point of producing individuals who are adaptable to change. If
il to educate individuals to live in a rapidly changing society
then they will not be able to deal effectively with the flexible future.

... The major block to improving public education is not financial
support, as entrenched interests advocate. The major obstacle is the
rigid organization that has been even further regimented by
scheduling students into a certain number of periods within a
particular grade rather than into a desirable program of studies.
Conventional school scheduling seems to have been designed largely
for the purpose of getting students out of the hall at certain times.
The result is a 'misfit' brand of education, which is being
administered to large numbers of students. The idea of placement in
a curriculum appropriate to the individual, however, is much more
than just a change in the organizational process. It advocates a shift
in the intent of the educational program. The changed direction
comprises a giant step from rigidity toward extreme flexibility. The
Appropriate Placement school champions a move from a curriculum
for the group to a curriculum for the individual. At the far end of the
swing of the nongraded pendulum is the exotic concept of learning
so highly individualized that some students will receive their
education by appointment.

An open classroom requires flexibility in the grouping of
children for instruction. Groupings must be based on the needs
of children regardless of age or grade (See following illustration).
Teachers should be assigned to groups according to their own
backgrounds, interests and abilities. Some teachers prefer working with slower children, while others prefer those with faster
learning rates.

Because the concern is with meeting individual needs,
flexibility in grouping is required. Grouping children on the
basis of chronological age for an entire year will not provide the
proper educational experiences to meet varied and ever-
changing needs of individuals. Not only are there differences in
needs, but also differences in rates and styles of learning.

The needs of each individual are constantly changing; therefore, grouping must change as needs change. Imperative to the success of open classrooms is the development of a flexible concept of school organization to provide a more desirable quality of learning for each student.

A flexibly organized school is somewhat like a big, one-room schoolhouse, but with many teachers. In the one-room school it was not only natural but necessary to depend considerably upon individualized instruction. There was such a range of ability and interest among children of widely varying ages and maturity that any kind of grouping was almost impossible.

As enrollments increased and subgrouping became necessary,

the division was made by considering chronological age and physical size: thus, the establishment of the graded school. Children were grouped according to grade. There was not much correlation between chronological age and scholastic achievement; however, the subject matter was sequentially organized by grades and the complexity increased as the child advanced through school.

Almost from the beginning of the graded structure educators have been concerned with trying to provide for individual differences. They have experimented with many grouping schemes in an effort to facilitate learning. Pupils have been grouped according to chronological age, sex, mental test scores, interests, behavior, and various combinations of these indexes. Regardless of the scheme tried, the results seem to be the same old problem of providing for the individual learner. B. Frank Brown also states, "The graded organization is like an ice tray guaranteed to freeze into rigidity everything that is put into it. Iconoclasts have condemned it as 'a cage for every age.' "[3]

The open classroom is a return to the philosophy of the one-room schoolhouse. Each individual needs physical activity; he needs to talk; he needs to be part of a small group; he needs time to work alone; he needs creative activities; he needs some large group experiences; he needs to be himself.

In an open classroom one might see the following activities happening simultaneously: the teacher working with an instructional group (eight to twelve children) on a particular skill that is a common need of all those in this group (See Figure 2-3); a group of children listening to a story record with headphones (See Figure 2-4); a parent volunteer and a group involved in a discussion of various readings on a particular topic; an aide sitting with a group as they share library stories; a child typing his own story; several children writing letters (See Figure 2-5);

[3]B. Frank Brown, *The Nongraded High School*, © 1963, p. 27. Reprinted by permission of Prentice-Hall, Inc., Englewood Cliffs, N.J.

others working independently at learning stations with programmed material; a group in the "living room" corner writing
poetry (See Figure 2-6); some children reading just for pleasure
(See Figure 2-7); one child helping another with sight vocabulary (See Figure 2-8); three boys building a miniature space ship—
the activities are limitless.

Figure 2-3

Figure 2-4

Figure 2-5

Figure 2-6

Figure 2-7

Figure 2-8

Each child has the freedom to choose from a variety of alternatives as his needs change or as he completes an activity. Each day is different—each activity is different—but all of these experiences are meaningful because they are real to the child and are satisfying to his needs.

Continuous Learning

Continuous learning is not a product; it is a process—a lifelong process from birth to death. This concept is a continuum over which it is possible to move toward a complete fulfillment of the goal of individualized learning. As a process it includes many choices for school organization: team teaching; large-group and small-group instruction; flexible scheduling; instructional uses of data processing; independent study; use of educational media; techniques for evaluation—all of which are integral components of the open classroom.

In order to keep continuous education at the center of curriculum development, values must be articulated, meanings must be explicit and descriptive terms must be substantiated so that there will be mutual understanding. We must work toward the goal of making learning highly individualized to meet the needs of each at every stage throughout the learning process.

An infant responds to objects and events in his home environment. Very early in life he hears, sees, touches and manipulates. He soon learns that crying will satisfy his need for food. These experiences provide him with background for organizing sounds into a sensible pattern, which eventually become words. These words, associated with direct experience, are soon spoken with meaning.

Noticing things and listening to the correctly spoken words that describe them helps the preschool child develop vocabulary and speech. These direct experiences of seeing, hearing, feeling, manipulating, listening and speaking lead quickly into reading, writing and spelling.

Teachers should plan to use many direct experiences with children in working with words. All children do not come from the same background or home environment; they have not all had the same experiences. They do not all develop language abilities in the same sequence or at the same chronological age. One child does not read as well at age ten as another does at age eight.

Reading activities must be made interesting and meaningful throughout the entire elementary program. For reading instruction to be most meaningful, teachers must consider individual differences in learning ability and previous experience. Instruction must proceed from the familiar to the new, from the easy to the more difficult.

At the beginning levels, concrete experiences should be used to build meanings and aid the child in learning basic sight words. The best source of teaching material is the child's own experiences. Use the language-experience approach. In order to help the child achieve independence in learning new words and reading with meaning, the teacher must help him develop the skills of using context clues and phonetic and structural analysis.

As the child progresses and reaches higher levels, the major aim of reading instruction is to prepare him for reading particular materials. Also, it seeks to establish independence in using work-analysis skills, deriving correct meaning and reading for specific purposes (textbook assignments in locating, organizing and evaluating information, etc.).

Teachers must continuously analyze how well each child reads and what his deficiencies are, prescribe appropriate learning activities, provide instructional materials suited to the needs of each and evaluate each child's progress so that deficiencies can be overcome (See Figure 2-9).

Continuous appraisal of each child's progress enables the teacher to ascertain strengths and weaknesses, provide a variety of appropriate learning activities and select the most effective instructional materials. This appraisal of each child's ability and achievement is necessary to provide for individual differences. Also, it organizes learning activities that will enable each child to make continuous progress commensurate with his own rate and style as he moves through the elementary, middle, high school and college programs and into adult continuing education.

GOALS AND OBJECTIVES OF THE CURRICULUM

The curriculum in the open classroom must be broad and flexible to meet the challenges and interests of all the students. The heart of the curriculum should be the development of a child's mental thought process while the body of current knowledge should serve only as the vehicle. Whenever there is a sequence of instructional skills, it should be followed. Opportunity for self-acceptance and self-discovery is the essence for making the curriculum real and meaningful.

The curriculum, then, becomes an organized series of experiences that has been decided upon in terms of the needs of the learner. This provides for his continuous growth and development toward desirable goals or behavioral objectives. The purpose of these learning activities is to enable the child, under the direction of the school, to acquire and develop skills, abilities, understandings and attitudes that will help him live effectively and happily in his environment.

Using a Variety of Instructional Materials

The program in the open classroom is not geared to the basal textbook approach. Teachers use a variety of materials including trade books, paperbacks, tapes, records, films, filmstrips, experience stories, concrete materials, programmed materials, etc., as well as basal texts.

The teacher selects the material that will best satisfy each instructional need. The materials vary from day to day. A child or an instructional group does not use the same text day after day and page after page. Instead, he uses only that section on a certain day to meet a particular need.

The following is a suggested list of materials, equipment and space that should be available to the open classroom:

- large collection of library books
- large collection of paperbacks
- work space for showing a film or examining a map
- conference space for groups to meet
- files of textbooks, manuals, workbooks and teaching guides
- typing and duplicating facilities
- filmstrips
- quiet work space with reference materials available
- recordings (tape and disc)
- slides and transparencies
- maps, charts, globes, graphs
- small, quiet areas for independent study
- single-concept films (film loops)
- slide projector
- single-concept projector
- 8mm sound projector
- 8mm or Super-8 movie camera
- polaroid camera
- tape recorders
- filmstrip previewers
- opaque projector
- headphone sets

- filmstrip projectors
- 16mm movie sound projectors
- overhead projectors
- record players
- work space with water for art work
- variety of art media
- outdoor space for nature study, gardening and free play.

Figure 2-9

The teacher should include in her plans a complete list of sources of materials that will be needed to fully develop every individual and group activity that is to be undertaken. There are basically two types of materials necessary: those that are used primarily to help the individual child and those that are used to help a group of children understand important things that come up in group activities. In selecting these materials the teacher should make certain that they will benefit those using them by helping them grow.

Promoting Creativity

The philosophy of the open classroom is enhanced by the encouragement of diversity and creativity. Through this encouragement, the individual has a chance to be himself without coercion from others. A diversity of groups and activities gives him the opportunity to find himself at ease in the groups that satisfy his needs.

Creativity means action. Each individual has within him some creative power. Regardless of the quantity, quality or form of expression, it can contribute to an attitude about living. In open classrooms we need to provide an ever-increasing variety of activities that will provide opportunities for individuals to express their ideas, imaginations and experiences (See Figure 2-10).

Motivation comes from the satisfaction of seeing one's ideas take on meaning. A simple way to encourage and promote creativity is to use the experience-story approach. Have a child tell you a story of one of his experiences and you write it for him. Another way to begin is to read or tell the first half of a story and ask the child to complete it. You may prefer to show a picture and have the child tell you about it. If you are working with a group you could make an oral statement and have them take turns adding lines to the story. You might make a collection and set up a "junk" table of old pieces and parts of things and see what the children make with these. Have all sorts of paints and other art materials available.

Remember, creativity means activity. The open classroom should be a "doing" place.

Figure 2-10

GUIDELINES FOR DEVELOPING THE CURRICULUM
FOR THE OPEN CLASSROOM

In planning the curriculum to focus on the individual, the following guidelines should be kept in mind:

1. There are differences as well as similarities among individuals.
2. Learning is evidenced through a change in behavior.

3. The most meaningful learning takes place through the process of discovery of one's creative potency.

4. Individuals draw relationships from their background of experiences.

5. Individuals react to stimuli and initiate action at their own rates and depths.

6. Learning takes place best when the individual has the freedom of choice.

7. Each child is in the continual process of individual growth.

8. Each child has rights and responsibilities as an individual.

9. Each child has rights and responsibilities as a member of a group.

10. There is a direct relationship between meaningful learning and amount of personal involvement.

11. Learning situations need to be provided at many levels in a variety of groupings.

12. The school environment must be one that encourages a feeling of belonging.

13. Each child must have opportunities to think and work as an individual as well as a member of a group.

14. Learning takes place best when an individual assumes responsibility for his own program of instruction.

—SUMMARY—

Curriculum for the open classroom includes arranging school facilities, providing materials, managing social relationships and activities to promote worthwhile and productive living for children.

Most human learning is not the result of instruction; rather, it is the result of the interrelationships of human beings as they develop in social situations.

We must be sincerely concerned about the welfare of each child and accept him for what he is. We can provide flexible grouping, one-to-one situations, or independent study and call this individualized instruction—but what we should really be concerned about is individualized learning. Regardless of the teaching alternatives we provide, the learning that takes place is by each individual.

The open classroom should be child-centered and should recognize the importance of the interest of the learner and his involvement in planning his own activities.

We need a vastly enriched environment that allows children to explore with concrete materials and to interact with others. Children learn best when they are following their own interests or questioning their own experiences.

Freedom is the power of effective choice; choice demands viable alternatives. Freedom is a mental attitude; it is not an end in itself, but a means by which thinking, judging, evaluating and acting may be integrated into the development of individual capacity.

In the open classroom freedom should be *for* instruction, not *from* instruction. This new freedom is toward self-direction and self-discipline. Emphasis must be on learning (what pupils actually do) rather than on instruction (what is done for pupils).

The needs of each individual are constantly changing; therefore, groupings must change as needs change. Imperative to the success of open classrooms is the development of a flexible concept of school organization to provide a more desirable quality of learning for each student.

Continuous learning is not a product; it is a lifelong process from birth to death. This concept is a continuum over which it is possible to move toward a complete fulfillment of the goal of individualized learning. As a process it includes many choices for school organization: team teaching; large-group and small-group instruction; flexible scheduling; instructional uses of data processing; independent study; use of educational media; techniques for evaluation—all of which are integral components of the open classroom.

The philosophy of the open classroom is enhanced by the encouragement of diversity and creativity. Through this encouragement, the individual has a chance to be himself without coercion from others. A diversity of groups and activities gives him the opportunity to find himself at ease in the groups that satisfy his needs. The open classroom is a "doing" place.

chapter three || The Administrator and the Open Classroom

Although there will always be a need for imaginative and well-prepared superintendents and other top-level administrators and supervisors, the most crucial need is to have highly capable administrators at the building level.

THE EDUCATIONAL LEADER

The principal is the key to providing more meaningful learning for children. He must have faith in the staff and be able to free teachers of unnecessary pressures so that they can carry out their important responsibilities to the children.

The principal sets the "tone" of the school; and the atmosphere he creates must be relaxed. The principal, as the educational leader in the school, must enthusiastically accept the responsibility of creating an atmosphere that will free teachers so that they may contribute to the leadership process.

The whole school must be filled with the cooperative approach to common problems—those which affect the way of life in the school and community.

Cooperative leadership necessitates interaction within the school. All those who are concerned and affected by decisions should share in the making of those decisions. A school needs the leadership of values and ideas rather than the leadership of authoritarian position or job title.

The morale of each staff member is strengthened when he feels that his ideas and suggestions are welcomed and respected. School policies should be thought of as "ours" rather than "his." The behavior of a teacher is controlled by the values that are shaped by her experiences; therefore, she is more likely to work creatively with children when the school is permeated with the cooperative approach.

The principal should approach any change enthusiastically, but also carefully, so that teachers' security will not be threatened. Often, his role in initiating change is determined by the readiness of the staff to assume its share of responsibility in the change process.

The principal must possess skill in leading group discussions and know how to work honestly and sincerely with others so that the creative power of each is freed to make contributions to the goals of the group. He must be sensitive to the attitudes, values, and needs of each. It is the responsibility of the principal to conduct himself in such a way that he exemplifies desirable educational values. His behavior should reflect sound human values, a well-adjusted personality and a positive outlook on life. Above all, he should be enthusiastic in his role as the educational leader.

Supervisory Responsibilities

Supervision is a form of continual in-service responsibility in which supervision becomes both an end and a means to an end for teachers. In this sense, it is a service: an in-service function for teachers. The most meaningful task for the supervisor and the teacher to work on together is improving the classroom teacher-student relationship.

The primary role of the building principal is that of instructional leader. The principal is the supervisor; he is responsible for the educational program in his school. The theory of supervision to be presented here should enable a principal to assert himself with greater success in the areas of evaluation and staff relations in working toward the goal of improving teaching behavior. For many reasons, school principals spend an insufficient amount of time and effort on their most important responsibility: continuous professional education. The principal should provide leadership to the field of educational administration to the same degree that teachers provide teaching techniques and beliefs that are exemplary for the profession. Although there are many exceptions, most of the desirable innovations that have originated in schools have come about in spite of the principals—not because of them.

This must change! There is a dominance of administrative managers and efficiency experts among the ranks of principals. Their time is spent on those tasks that have to do with the routine running of the school. Although these functions are important, the principal must concentrate his efforts on the instructional program; for the future of education must be guided by the educational leader.

Researchers have attempted to identify the critical elements of leadership behavior. In most of the research, there seems to be a common element: an emphasis on human relationships. Human relations is the crux of the whole matter. To recognize this is one thing; to pay the price of commitment is another. The school principal is in a relatively good position to change the total pattern of instruction and thus open minds of teachers and students. This can be done, but it can only be done when it is seen as being of primary value.

The characteristics of a good teacher-student relationship apply equally to a good principal-teacher relationship. Principals co-working with teachers can help change negative conditions in the classroom if they keep this in mind. The improving of relationships in the classroom is as much the task of the principal as it is the task of the teacher.

Education can best be improved by the leadership of ideas and values; and the principal must provide this creative leadership in working with teachers. A school staff is a community of educators, each sensitive to the needs, feelings and attitudes of all the others. They need to plan, work, and evaluate cooperatively.

The principal should provide the kind of working environment that challenges teachers to look at school improvement objectively. Openness should prevail between faculty and administration and, although the principal should see that the climate is open, he should also be clever enough to challenge suggestions with sound alternatives, thus provoking deeper insights into the purposes for change.

Each staff needs to analyze the needs of the school and the community and together develop an organization that will create the best possible learning atmosphere to provide for the unique needs of each individual and to promote self-direction and self-discipline.

In-Service Programs

In-service education programs directed towards developing open classrooms must permit teachers to grapple with the problems essential to producing change in schools when pertinent questions are raised. The principal must recognize that these problems can no longer be dealt with in the traditional manner. New information concerning learning, curriculum structure, and child growth and development must be utilized in solving these problems in an objective way. In-service education should not attempt to force each teacher into the same mold, but should provide for developing teacher competencies in dealing with instructional problems and teaching strategies at each teacher's own level of sophistication.

In-service education requires time. Yet very often no time is allowed for the task of reorienting teachers to a new philosophical understanding of a changing school organization and developing new competencies in instructional procedures. Teachers are simply expected to extend their working hours for this purpose.

Administrators should also be concerned about the mental health of their teachers and should not expect them to put in long hours after the regular school day is over. Increased funds for extending the school year and for releasing teachers from regular classroom assignments for in-service education are essential to accomplishing the task of helping teachers to redefine their roles in the process of developing open classrooms for children.

The principal will need to acquire an understanding of the philosophy of the open classroom. He must be cognizant of individual differences within his staff. Therefore, he should help teachers identify their specific needs and seek to have them adopt in-service techniques that are appropriate for meeting these needs. He must not force all teachers into the same in-service mold.

There is a need for less-structured training programs with an emphasis on relating theory and practice in the school setting. This means a departure from the usual college-classroom lecture type of instruction to more emphasis on inquiry in seeking solutions to problems that require change.

Principals need to build for themselves—through conferences, inter-school visitation, reading, college seminars, etc.—a background of understanding of the open classroom so they can provide the necessary leadership for their staffs and for the community. One of the goals of the open classroom is that of teaching the students to program their own learning activities. The principal, too, must program his own learning so that he can give direction to his community and his staff. Good principals will never stand back to see which way the crowd is going. Instead, you'll find them out in front, leading the crowd.

Sample Bulletins for Teachers

One technique that a principal can use effectively to help his staff is to write bulletins for teachers. The bulletins should make specific suggestions for teachers to use in opening up their classrooms. Several such bulletins are offered here as examples.

BULLETIN

TO: Teachers
FROM: Principal
RE: Self-direction and Self-discipline

The social climate in the school should be such that each child and each group is encouraged to be self-directed and self-disciplined. Self-direction and self-discipline will not just happen. Children need to be taught how to effectively utilize their freedom.

To establish this kind of climate you should help the children by starting with small group work. Be patient and be willing to allow more time for these cooperative activities to show results. The process is more important than the product.

In organizing these small groups (4-8 children), those with similar interests should work together. Children who are already friends should be in the same group. Help each group set its goals and understand the purposes of its activity. Help each child to see what he can do in helping the group reach the goal. Continuous evaluation by the group will help accomplish the desired results.

As children develop skill as contributing members of small groups and as they become more secure in their feelings toward themselves as well as others, then larger group activities should be planned. It may be well to point out that group work is not the only method of helping children acquire self-direction and self-discipline. Many tasks must be undertaken on an individual basis. A group activity should be planned when there is a common need which could best be satisfied through a cooperative effort.

Children need to work together, to help each other, and to learn from each other. It is quite normal for children to talk over their experiences. It is also natural for children to talk with adults. You should expect and encourage children to interact as they live together at school. Children should not be expected to sit down and keep quiet.

Encourage children to participate in group planning, to think critically, and to initiate activities. Children's problems are solved by questioning, evaluating, and pooling of the ideas of the various members of the group. In such an environment, your role as teacher is that of a guide. You are the resource person—the "expert" in group leadership, but not necessarily the group leader.

BULLETIN

TO: Teachers
FROM: Principal
RE: Utilizing Peer Teachers

As you know, the behavior of a child at any age is strongly influenced by the opinions of his peers. Under the guidance of the teacher, children can enter constructively into the instructional phase of school life.

Peer teaching can be done successfully in several ways. Perhaps the easiest way is on a one-to-one basis. This works well in drill work where both need to practice the same thing—maybe some division facts. They could take turns in checking each other orally.

One-to-one situations are limitless. Another example might be one child listening to another give his campaign speech, which he has prepared for the student body in seeking the office of president of student council.

You could divide your room into many small groups (2 to 3 children) and have peer teachers from other rooms come in to give specific instruction. You could plan all the details with the peer teachers or you could simply give them the task and leave the selection of materials and methods to the students. This is a highly successful technique; children speak each other's language and they can often explain something to peers much more easily than adults can.

In another situation a child who is very good at oral reading might spend a few minutes reading orally to a peer group of less mature readers.

Experience has proven that many times the peer teacher is learning as much as, if not more than, those being taught. Also take note that a peer teacher is continuing to develop a positive self-concept as he participates in this leadership role.

BULLETIN

TO: Teachers
FROM: Principal
RE: The Group Process

Group unity does not just happen; it must be achieved. This group spirit will come as the result of everyone working and playing together—that is, "living" at school. This unity is not something concrete that you can put your hands on; it is something you can sense, feel, experience, and enjoy. It is the "style of living" in the school.

This group spirit is not an end in itself. Through the group process each child will continuously improve his methods of operation as an effective member of the group; he will continue to find satisfaction in the achievements of the group; he will continually realize and appreciate the values of togetherness in the activities of the school.

As teacher, you are in a position to provide many experiences that can best be accomplished by the group. By sharing the leadership role with different children, the group will derive satisfaction and pride in accomplishment. Guide children to plan their own activities and to put their own plans into action. Children should share the responsibility for keeping their room and school neat, clean, and attractive.

Committees should be responsible for planning social functions such as parties and assemblies. When children are responsible for the things that are important to them, they will respond with appropriate behavior. If the group process is utilized in activities and experiences that are relevant to children, then children will see the value of the democratic way of life.

As a specific example of this kind of experience I'm suggesting the organization of some kind of student government in each classroom.

BULLETIN

TO: Teachers
FROM: Principal
RE: Developing Sensitivity Through Role Playing

Dramatic play (role playing) is informal and creative portrayal of experience without a set pattern or memorization of parts. Play is a natural means of expression for children; it is a fundamental activity of childhood. Through play, children express themselves with whole-heartedness, sincerity, interest, and concentration. It is satisfying to them, and serves both as an outlet for expression and as a means for gaining new experiences.

In dramatic play individuals identify themselves with persons and objects and act out what they have experienced. This creates new interests, problems and needs. It contributes to the development of democratic group-action skills. In dramatic play children become cooperative, courteous, sensitive to the needs of others, responsible and tolerant of each other.

These activities will afford opportunities for you to observe children to gain insight into many aspects of child development and social learning. As children become absorbed in a given situation, they release tensions, feelings, and attitudes toward themselves and others. Growth in dramatic play is a steady progression from individual play to large-group play.

To begin such an activity, lead a discussion with the group about how you will read a "story" which is never finished; it just stops. Explain that they are to assume the roles of the characters and act out an ending.

Children will develop insights from discussion and enactments. These insights, which they may enlarge into generalizations, are the important learnings; such generalizations may guide them in making future decisions.

The goal is to achieve some growth on the children's part in sensitivity to other's feelings, and to achieve responses that reveal growth in personal integrity and group responsibility. If the group's response reveals that they are becoming increasingly aware of the humane issues involved in the social problems they are analyzing, if their choices indicate that they are choosing to support such issues, they are making important growth.

BULLETIN

TO: Teachers
FROM: Principal
RE: Providing Security for Children

Each child needs to have security. He needs to feel that he belongs because, as he is, he is important, needed and valued by everyone with whom he lives and learns.

You can help establish this security by being friendly. Each child needs to see you as a kind, understanding, and sympathetic adult interested in his well-being.

As teacher, you must sensitively recognize each child's

uniqueness and constructively build upon his differences instead of expecting him to fit into the same identical mold.

A permissive atmosphere must be in existence throughout the school, for such an environment will free each child to be himself. He needs to know that the teacher respects his individuality and has faith in him and in his potential. You must take time to listen to a child as he talks about his experiences, presents his problems, and asks his questions.

Show by your enthusiasm that you enjoy each child with whom you work. Plan the activities with the children in a democratic manner so that every one of them knows that his contributions are respected and important. All children should be given equal respect. Praise for achievement should be honest and should be related in terms of the goals and objectives previously established.

The greatest human resource to a child is his teacher. You must show a genuine affection for your pupils. I'm not implying that you need to baby the child by hugging and kissing; I'm suggesting that you should be "warm" toward children. Act like a human being. Live with the children; play with them; work with them; live with them.

Instead of acting out the stereotyped authoritarian role by giving all the orders and commands, assume the role of one of the members of the group; get in the children's camp, so to speak. Actions speak louder than words.

Take time to talk and listen to each child. This is a realistic way of showing a sincere affection, and it makes the child feel that he can always confide in a true friend.

In-Service Activities

The development of meaningful and integrated in-service education activities is crucial to the success of open classrooms. Following are some specific suggestions:

- Workshops can be designed to acquaint teachers and staff with materials and resources available to them for classroom use and for independent use by pupils. Workshops can provide teachers with the opportunity to plan for using materials in the classroom and to experiment with the operation of equipment.

- Seminars can serve to instruct teachers in a variety of areas. University consultants or other authorities can present ideas and lead discussions on a variety of topics such as:

    - conditions that allow learning;
    - social, physiological, and psychological factors that influence the pupil in the learning process;
    - attitudes and values of the teacher;
    - communicating with parents;
    - observing and evaluating pupil behavior;
    - using teacher aides.

- Brainstorming meetings can serve as a means for creating new and innovative ideas. These should provide teachers and consultants with opportunities to interact and exchange ideas about teaching and learning by utilizing small group meetings.
- T-group meetings can serve as opportunities for teachers to have permissive discussions about their feelings and attitudes toward teaching. In these "group-centered" discussions the teachers can discuss their attitudes and the impact they have on others.
- Sharing sessions offer opportunities for staff members to meet informally and to exchange ideas about instruction techniques, utilizing materials, etc. The leader of the sharing sessions could be the reading teacher, the team leader, or any classroom teacher.
- Demonstration lessons may be presented to the staff

members by consultants, reading teachers, principals, or teachers. These would be planned programs based upon teacher or staff request. Demonstrations would serve as a means of sharing new techniques, illustrating new materials, and showing how theory relates to practice. Demonstration lessons could be performed before an individual teacher or before a group of teachers.

- Displays of materials and other resources may be used for the purpose of promoting continued awareness and use of a variety of teaching aids in the classroom.
- Independent study should be utilized. Teachers may use the professional library, make visitations, and meet with specialists and consultants.
- As a part of the in-service education program for teachers, a professional library should be established. This would enhance teachers' independent study and would serve to supplement other in-service activities.

Improving Staff Morale

In creating good staff morale the principal must remember that teachers are human beings first and teachers second. Their emotions, habits of behavior and values are likely to determine their conduct more than verbalizing about educational philosophy.

Human nature can be modified, but this requires time, effort, and well-designed modifying experiences. If the principal is patient and works for gradual change, there will be less concern and greater satisfaction in the process than if a revolutionary plan is used. Take the easiest problems first. If teachers have opportunities to solve relatively simple problems first they may develop skills and enthusiasm for problem-solving before confronted with more complicated ones.

It is a fact of human behavior that one tends to repeat that which is pleasant and to avoid that which is unpleasant. Make school experiences pleasant. A sense of humor helps create good working conditions, which can serve to good purposes in developing a rewarding school environment. Coffee breaks, duty-free lunch periods with opportunities for recreation—for example, Ping-Pong—will work wonders in improving staff morale. The simplest way to put it is: treat teachers as human beings.

PRINCIPAL-SCHOOL BOARD RELATIONSHIPS

Boards of education play important roles in creating favorable public attitudes toward the work of the school in general and the program of instruction in particular. Traditionally, local boards of education have been the policy-making bodies for the entire system. They have operated almost independently from all other community agencies and without advice and suggestions from anyone else. Conditions are changing rapidly and, as a result, there is much more community involvement in the decisions that affect the educational system today.

The principal is a key member in the educational leadership team. It is his responsibility to interpret school board policies to the community, and he has an equal obligation to keep the school board informed of the instructional program of the school as well as the demands of society upon the school. As the liason between the school board, teachers, parents, pupils and the community, the principal must inspire the school board members to examine carefully the total social scene. In his relationships with board members, the principal should aspire to a cooperative raising of sights to meet the needs of today's society.

PRINCIPAL-COMMUNITY RELATIONSHIPS

Community involvement has caused the school to become the center of community life; but schools are not the only institutions that provide learning opportunities. Many activities are provided by church groups, recreation departments, community associations, and volunteer groups and individuals.

The principal must develop the skill of seeing the role of education in the whole social scene and help develop the concept of the community school. This concept is an attempt to infuse an authentic community life into a building that heretofore had been locked and darkened during after-school hours. A school should be a place where the learning process is continually evolving, not just a building where children come for five or six hours a day and are then released to shift for themselves to find fun and entertainment.

In addition to its obvious role as a learning institution, the school should be a focal point of the community. All parents look to education as the key to the dreams and aspirations they hold for their children; but all too many times education is thwarted in youth because children feel a certain alienation from the institution. Often the school does not have the warmth and security of home, and the transition for the child can be too harsh and difficult to accept. It is this situation that creates the potential high school dropout. The only way to combat this is to make the school a living, breathing part of the everyday experience of each member of the community, by bringing the parents into the school, making them a part of it, and giving them an investment in it, both intellectually and emotionally.

If the school building squats unused and deserted during after-school hours and if we believe that the school building belongs to the people of the community, then it *really* should belong to them. The school must be a live, breathing part of the community so that the community will be a much better place in which to live. This is the philosophy of the open classroom.

INTERPERSONAL RELATIONSHIPS

The people who are part of a school organization have interrelationships that depend upon the nature of schools as social systems. Human values are central to educational leadership.

The basic ways of viewing people are applicable to all individuals regardless of the roles they play. The school has goals it is attempting to meet. Individuals within the school bring with them their own background of experiences and their own responses to the roles they enact, and they will be seeking self-fulfillment in the enactment of their roles. The extent to which this highest human value can be attained by an individual as part of a school system will determine the quality of his performance in his assignment.

The principal who seeks to become a great educational leader must realize that his success will depend upon the group of individuals with whom he works closely. He should see that a climate is established in which the creative talents of all members of the school staff will be released and coordinated.

Although the school may treat pupils as members of groups, the learning that takes place is individual. In many school systems, however, the emphasis has remained upon instruction (what is done for pupils) rather than upon learning (what pupils actually do).

Establishing the total school program and climate to make it possible for students to attain self-actualization requires a team approach. The total staff must participate in all activities and planning. Before a school can expect to have students experience self-actualization it must be certain that it is providing opportunities for the student to attain feelings of belonging.

Students are persons who are enacting roles in a school situation. The educational program should bring the school's expectation of student roles and the students' own expectations into close harmony. We need to use the students' own values for continuing guidance in decision-making that will lead both pupils and teachers toward more meaningful approaches to relationships with each other. The emphasis should be upon learning by the pupils, with student self-control a number-one goal.

The determination of how good the schools in a community will be depends upon how deeply the people want good schools, upon their willingness to become involved in providing good education and their willingness to pay for it. The relationships of the principal with the various publics involve two-way communication. He can find guidelines for his behavior in the values of a free society. Among these values is the concept that the school must be the servant of the people: the goals are to be set by the people. A major responsibility for the principal is to involve the community in planning, operating and evaluating the school program. To meet this responsibility the principal must, of course, be an expert in human relations.

Figure 3-1 illustrates an organizational plan for providing opportunities for this two-way communication. In this plan the principal is the center of the educational program. He is assisted by a representative council, which meets regularly with him to offer ideas and suggestions from parent groups, administration, community groups, teaching staff and pupils. This model shows one realistic way of having all those influenced by the school program become involved in making decisions concerning the program.

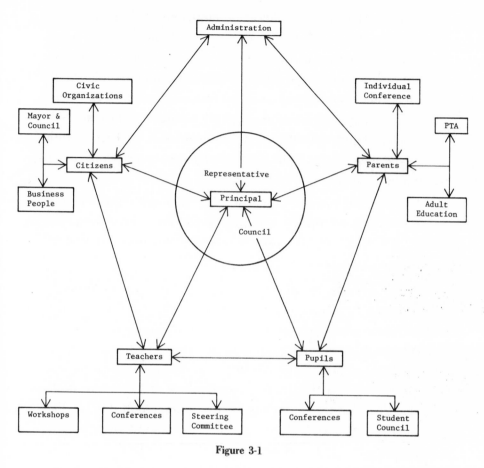

Figure 3-1

—SUMMARY—

As the educational leader, the principal has many supervisory responsibilities—the first and foremost being to the children whom the school serves. The school was instituted for the purpose of serving children's needs, and teachers need to be constantly reminded that the children should receive primary consideration when decisions are made.

Knowing the basic patterns of development of children is also the responsibility of the principal: he should have a basic knowledge of the nature of their surroundings and home conditions. With this, the principal should know and understand the teachers on his staff and the factors that motivate their behavior. Unless the leader knows each member of the staff as a total personality, it will be difficult for him to have a full understanding of the needs, urges, and drives of the people he is supposed to lead.

Another important facet of the principal's job is his understanding of the community which the school seeks to serve, for each school exists in a social environment that is unique to that school.

If the schools are to serve as one of the agencies through which society attempts to improve itself, educators must understand what constitutes societal development, in what directions it is tending to go, and how the schools may help in this development. It is particularly important that the principal be equipped to participate in group thinking that concerns itself with social change, for as the leader, he is responsible for the level of professional discussion and for its effectiveness. If staff meetings are to be productive and satisfactorily run, the principal must know when and under what circumstances his leadership is needed and how the group members may be helped to achieve their best thinking.

The principal is responsible for the proper guidance of research activities; he should possess the ability to help teachers see the opportunities for discovering local needs for research on such problems as placement, promotion, reporting to parents, beginning reading activities, evaluation, etc. In addition to this, the principal actually coordinates all the activities of all members of the staff. A total school "family" is composed of classroom teachers, custodians, nurses, librarians, cafeteria workers, specialists, visiting teachers, supervisors, teacher aides, secretaries, volunteers, parents and pupils. If the program is to be of maximum benefit to children, it is imperative that all the people concerned with their development be guided in a coordinated effort.

To assure adequate planning and effective execution of plans for curriculum development, the principal must be able to provide guidance to the group through his understanding of what constitutes the curriculum and how it may be developed.

The principal must exemplify in his behavior the democratic values he hopes will motivate teachers and students. Thus, he must act on democratic values instead of merely verbalizing about them, and he must accept the philosophy of the open classroom as his "way of life."

chapter four

The Teacher and the Open Classroom

The teacher is the most important factor in the development of an open classroom (See Figure 4-1). Children look to the teacher as an example, and they see how she lives more than they hear what she tells them to do.

Figure 4-1

Additional materials, newer buildings, smaller classes will not result in better schools unless teaching is improved. Thus, it becomes obvious that the key to successful open classrooms is quality teaching.

THE NATURE OF TEACHING

In his book, *The 8:10 Decision: Beginning Teaching*, John G. Boswell gives an excellent analysis of education, learning and teaching. He says:

> Teaching is the initiation, guiding, and assisting in evaluation of learning activities. Teaching a group of youngsters, usually 25 to 30, also involves some management of the social and physical environment. This assessment of the job a teacher does is at some variance with the traditional view of teaching. The teacher has been regarded as a repository of knowledge which he passed on to his students by telling them what he knew. In times past, when sources of information were limited, this was a major role of a teacher. The advent of the printing press has changed all of this. Not only are there more sources of information than one person can keep up with, there is also so much to know that one person cannot master any subject area.
>
> The teacher who attempts to act as a repository of knowledge for his students is constantly facing situations in which some student knows more than he does. This forces the teacher into the game of one-upmanship, or another game called dirty pool. In both these games, the teacher can be the only winner since both are always played with the student's score going into the gradebook.[1]

Instruction should be based upon diagnosis of individual needs. There should be continuous evaluation of each student so that his needs may be analyzed, learning activities may be

---

[1] John G. Boswell, *The 8:10 Decision: Beginning Teaching* (Washington, D.C.: The George Washington University, 1971) p. 21.

prescribed, and the proper materials may be provided to help him develop to his fullest potential. Teachers must provide learning activities that are relevant to the child; it is his right to understand the reason for each activity. When he needs the activity and sees how it is relevant to his way of life, the activity will become meaningful for him, and only then will he "learn."

Teaching is essentially the act of arranging school facilities, providing materials, managing social relationships and activities that will promote worthwhile and productive living for children.

Descriptions of Typical Teachers

If asked the question, "Who are our teachers?" my first reaction would be, "You name *it*; I've had *it* teaching in my school!"

• For example, there is Mr. X. By his actions he teaches hate, prejudice, violence, and lack of respect for the worth of the individual; he uses his classroom to vent his hate, frustration, and feelings of inadequacy. Pupils who come into contact with him are warped by the experience.

• Then there is Mr. Y. He does not make a positive contribution to pupil growth in the area of human relations; he acts more as a restrictive force to poor human relations. He prevents chaos; he has his class under control; he fights injustice; he protects the weak from the aggressive. He stops fights and attempts to prevent name-calling. Pupils do not increase in understanding, in sensitivity, in empathy, or in the skill of living more effectively with others as a result of their interaction with him; they are merely protected.

• Mrs. A does not oppose the development of group feeling. She finds that teaching is more fun for her when students like to be together. However, she believes group activity should be for things other than classwork. She encourages class parties and assembly programs, but when students begin classwork, each must work separately and decisions as to what should be done are the exclusive right and responsibility of the teacher.

• Mrs. B has all students follow the same course of study and work as a total class during each class period. Although all are given the same assignment, it is possible for a student to get specific help or an adaptation of the task if requested; she does consider individual differences within the framework of the prescribed curriculum.

• Mr. Z is a teacher because he gets a check at the end of the month. He doesn't bother to learn the names of all the students and doesn't want to know anything about them. He assigns the work to be done. The "good ones" do it, and they are given a passing grade. The "bad ones" can't or won't work at the required level and are failed. He thinks everything is fair and objective. All are treated alike; all are given the same assignments. Each student determines his own fate.

• Mrs. C has a minimum number of hours for certification and follows the textbooks to make uniform assignments. During class periods, pupils may ask questions, however. They may even suggest ideas that are not in the text and the teacher will spend time with them and the class. Products of student work are displayed and marks do not depend entirely upon ability to recall the facts in the book; some credit is given for being able to express the idea in the student's own words.

• Mrs. D plans what is to be done by the class, but students are allowed to suggest extra activities. A few minutes each day are taken to discuss items that have arisen during the day.

Occasionally the teacher has a conference with a pupil who is having difficulty to see what plans can be made to increase the pupil's effectiveness.

• I must tell you about Mr. R. He gets to school at the very last minute and leaves as early as possible. He avoids faculty meetings if possible and sits quietly when he is forced to attend. At the present time his primary interests are fishing, bridge and the part-time job tending bar. He feels that teachers are a boring lot and he doesn't want to associate with them.

• Then there's good old Mrs. E. She comes to school early, leaves late, and takes lots of work home with her. She operates a good self-contained classroom in a traditional manner. Her pupils always score well on standardized tests, but they are not permitted to participate with children from other rooms in any activities. She takes pride in "her" children and she doesn't want them to become contaminated by others.

• My last example is Mr. T. He has persuaded two other teachers to team with him in working with about 105 students. They plan together, teach together, and evaluate together. The instructional program is planned with the children; individual needs are met because of the flexibility in scheduling; each child is respected as an important human being. This team has created a democratic atmosphere in which diversity and creativity is encouraged. The children are really "turned on" because they plan, schedule and evaluate their own work; they really like school. Incidently, these children always score well on standardized tests. More importantly, they are involved in all school activities and are really learning how to live as they learn.

These examples of the variety of "our teachers" give evidence of the fact that there are also individual differences among teachers. Each has his own self-concept, his own ideas about school, his ideas about how to teach and what to teach.

BASIC PRINCIPLES OF THE LEARNING PROCESS

Learning is an individual matter. Each pupil is a unique human being with purposes of his own and a pattern of growth that he must follow in order to develop his feelings and his attitudes because his living demands this.

Learning is a continual process by which each person adjusts to his environment in a meaningful way. Each organizes and reorganizes his experiences into more meaningful behavior. The basic principles of the learning process include the following:

- there are differences as well as similarities among individuals;
- learning is evidenced through a change in behavior;
- the most meaningful learning takes place through the process of discovery of one's potency;
- individuals draw relationships from their background of experiences;
- individuals react to stimuli and initiate action at their own rates and depths;
- learning takes place best when the individual has the freedom of choice;
- each is in the continual process of individual growth;
- there is a direct relationship between meaningful learning and amount of personal involvement;
- learning takes place best when an individual assumes responsibility for his own program of instruction.

Definition of Quality Teaching

The greatest human resource to a child is his teacher, and this important adult must show a genuine affection for his pupils. I am not implying that we need to baby the child by hugging and kissing. I am suggesting that the teacher should be "warm" toward children. Teachers should act like human beings; they should live with the children; play with them; work with them; learn with them.

Instead of acting out the stereotyped authoritarian role by giving all the orders and commands, assume the role of one of the members of the group; get in the children's camp, so to speak. Through requests and suggestions as a member of the group, a teacher will reap higher rewards than through authoritarian commands. Take time to talk and listen to each child. This is a realistic way of showing sincere affection, and it makes the child feel that he can always confide in a true friend.

Each child needs to have security. He needs to feel that he belongs because, as he is, he is important, needed and valued by everyone with whom he lives and learns. The teacher can help establish this security by being friendly. Each child needs to see the teacher as a kind, understanding and sympathetic adult interested in his well-being. The teacher must sensitively recognize each child's uniqueness and constructively build upon his differences instead of expecting him to fit into some preconceived mold.

A permissive atmosphere must exist throughout the school, for such an environment will free each child to be himself. He needs to know that the teacher respects his individuality and has faith in him and in his potential. Teachers must take time to listen to a child as he talks about his experiences, presents his problems, and asks his questions.

An understanding teacher should show, by her enthusiasm, that she enjoys each child with whom she works. She should plan the activities with the children in a democratic manner so that every one of them knows that his contributions are respected and important.

Figure 4-2

The teacher must also recognize aggressiveness, withdrawal, or antisocial behavior as acts of insecurity and find ways other than punishment to help the child become secure.

Children look to teachers for guidance in the solution of their everyday problems; and they expect teachers to be able to understand and help solve the problems of group living. Caring must be the teacher's "style of living."

Utilizing the Group Process

Group unity does not just happen; it must be achieved. This group spirit will come as a result of everyone working and playing together—that is, "living" at school. This unity is not something concrete; it is something you can sense, feel, experience and enjoy. It is the "style of living" in open classrooms. Group spirit is not, however, an end in itself. Through the group process each child will continually improve his methods of operation as an effective member of the group; he will continue to find satisfaction in the achievements of the group; he will continually realize and appreciate the values of togetherness in the activities of the school.

Figure 4-3

The teacher should provide experiences that can best be accomplished by the group. By sharing the leadership role with different children, the group will derive satisfaction and pride in accomplishments. Guide children to plan their own activities and to put their own plans into action. For example, they should share the responsibility for keeping their school neat, clean, and attractive.

Committees are effective in planning social functions such as parties and assemblies. When children are responsible for the things that are important to them, they will respond with appropriate behavior. If the group process is utilized in activities and experiences that are relevant to children, children will see the value of the group process and become self-directed and self-disciplined.

Providing for Individual Differences

Meeting individual differences is not a technique; it is a way of living—a style of life. It includes accepting others, respecting their contributions, working for the kind of group operation in which each individual knows he has a part, and encouraging each child to give his best in each situation.

Many early childhood teachers provide opportunities for the children to talk about the plans for the day and help decide as a group. Each child's comments are seriously considered; consequently, each begins to feel important as a group member. Teachers provide many play activities, thus permitting observation of children so the teacher can recognize the problems, needs and strengths of each individual.

Many activities are interest-based so that the child can choose that which he wants to do. Those with similar interests can be grouped together.

Most teachers are aware of the fact that the greatest similarity among elementary children is the need for socialization. Activities such as talking, dramatizing, and playing games are encouraged. These activities are not just for "socializing"; they are also very important in language and cognitive development. Children learn as they live, play, and work together (See Figure 4-4).

Figure 4-4

As stated, learning is evidenced through a change in behavior. The emotional climate of a learning situation determines how well the pupil will obtain functional behavioral changes. Unless the emotional content of the situation is conducive to the acceptance of new information, that information will appear irrelevant and will be rejected. In every situation, boys and girls are striving to feel right about themselves, to feel that they have worth, to feel that they are accepted.

A child's own objectives are very important. Education and development have to interact. The goals must emerge from the activities rather than be predetermined from higher head-quarters.

More and more teachers are writing behavioral objectives. Taking into consideration the child's own goals, the teacher's objectives describe: 1) to what the child is to respond, 2) what observable behavior is anticipated or expected and, 3) what is the minimum level to be accepted. Educators seem to be moving away from long-range objectives to specific behavioral objectives to try to provide that which is best for each child, or group, at a particular point in time.

Individuals draw relationships from their background of experiences. The child does not need to sit down at a desk to "learn." All of his experiences, and particularly his first, should be ones in which he can see that teachers trust him and have faith in him. He should see at the very beginning that learning is not separate from living, but that he learns as he lives, at school as well as at home and in the community.

The language-experience approach is a good example to illustrate what many teachers are doing to utilize a child's background of experience. The child sees relevance in language activities because the story he reads is the story he wrote. Another example here is the utilization of field trips that provide experiences on which to base other activities. Teachers should attempt to plan school activities to relate to the child's background.

Individuals react to a stimulus and initiate action at their own rate and depth. Every child has the potential for many types of growth, but some of these potentials lie dormant throughout life, while others are developed in part. The determination of which possibilities are realized and the degree to which any is fulfilled are the functions of one's environment.

Figure 4-5

Teachers are more and more providing "things" for children to play with, experiment with, talk about, and generalize about. They are providing more opportunities for the child to think, to explore, and to discover. Flexibility is a major consideration in school organization, and the individualized instruction used in many school programs takes into consideration the fact that each individual has his own learning mode and developmental pattern. All are not expected to do the same "page" or even the same activity.

Each child must have opportunities to think and work as a member of a group as well as individually. The determination of group direction and policy is based upon the individual decisions of group members. If the society is to improve, or even sustain itself, its individual members must be able to make wise decisions. Each must be able to decide for himself what he values, what he wants, and what is the best method of obtaining it.

Not only does the pupil need to be a part of a group, but also to feel that his uniqueness is important and respected. The school should not only tolerate, but also encourage diversity and creativity. Through this encouragement, the individual child has a chance to be himself without coercion from others. A diversity of groups and activities in school gives him the opportunity to find himself at ease in the groups that satisfy his needs. He needs a variety of activities and a variety of groups. His way of living is multi-directional; he cannot survive if directed into uniformity.

Many teachers are providing opportunities for more group activities based on individual interests (See Figure 4-6). Children who are already friends are allowed and encouraged to be in the same group. Teachers are helping groups to set goals and to understand the purposes of their activity.

As a result, more and more children are solving their problems by questioning, evaluating, and pooling the ideas of the various members of the group, with the teacher assuming the role of a guide. She is becoming the resource person—the "expert" in group leadership, but not necessarily the group leader. This diversity of groups and activities gives each child the opportunity to find himself at ease in the groups that satisfy his needs.

Learning takes place best when an individual assumes responsibility for his own program of instruction. The child

Figure 4-6

needs to share the leadership responsibility; he needs to be a part of the decision-making process, to help set up his own goals and to evaluate his own progress. Children learn to play games, ride bikes, walk, run, and so on, without adult teachers telling them every move to make. They learn by *doing*. Children need only for the teacher to "free" them to teach themselves.

Many schools are beginning to utilize learning centers (See Figure 4-7). Through the utilization of learning stations and centers a child can work independently with a series of related activities designed to promote independent understanding of certain concepts. Ultimately, the child will develop the ability to schedule himself and discipline himself to carry out his own activities.

Learning to Learn

Learning to learn refers to a child's acquiring a method of solving problems. This phenomenon is becoming, and should

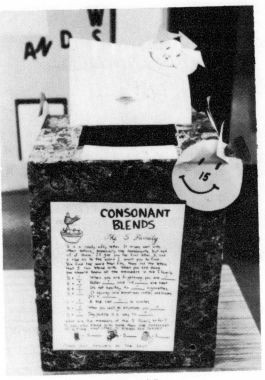

Figure 4-7

become, more prominent as an area of study in child development. The modern point of view about learning tends to regard
it as a variety of processes taking place within the learner. These
processes include coding, retrieval, categorizing, and labeling.
The learner approaches each new task with a collection of
previously acquired skills and concepts. He learns how to
organize that which he knows so that he can use this knowledge
in future learning tasks.

In the "learning to learn" phenomenon, instruction becomes
not a matter of communicating something to be stored, but a
matter of stimulating the learner to use his capabilities to
approach a new learning task. The focus here is on problem-
solving.

Children tend to "be like the teacher." The teacher becomes a "model." Once the role of model has been established, the teacher should "think out loud" her own behaviors. Example: "How did I get this answer? I guess I did this or that (specify). Now why did I do that?" etc. This will cause the child to try to think out his own process and he will soon realize that *he* is in charge of his own behavior.

Teachers should concentrate on the process rather than content. Instead of the teacher "covering" the material, the students should "uncover" it (See Figure 4-8). Teachers should plan concrete and specific physical experiences that clearly illustrate the concept and encourage the children to manipulate, experiment and formulate concepts. The curriculum should be closely related to the group's developing interests. Teachers should not be concerned about "finishing the book by June." The curriculum should emerge from the children.

Figure 4-8

Accordingly, the role of the teacher becomes that of a catalyst for learning—a guide, not a guard. Her contributions should be in providing materials and encouraging experimentation and discovery—not telling all the answers. Children are much more enthusiastic when given a chance to experiment and draw conclusions. This is learning to learn.

ROLE OF AFFECT IN EDUCATION

Human development is a process in which the human being is interacting with himself and his environment. Psychology has become so specialized that many have forgotten the *whole* human being. Our purpose is to look at the *total human being* over a *whole life span;* for the danger in dealing with young children is in emphasis on cognition (the idea itself) to the exclusion of the affective domain (the feeling or emotion attached to the idea).

Currently, there seems to be more interest in the affective side of development as an area of study. We see much more in writing about self-concept, socialization, values, etc., than we did a few years back.

Affect and cognition are inseparably related: each implies the other. For example, in the infancy period the child, through the acquisition of language (a cognitive task), learns to see himself as separate and unique from his environment. Thus, affect and cognition serve each other. The disequilibrium created from the transactions between internal growth and external social pressures acts as a motivating force for development. As the child incorporates aspects of the external world to fit his views and as he changes some of his ideas because of his contacts with reality, he grows in competence and self-esteem. At all ages, cognitive organization, development, and change are motivated by a search for meaning.

We have organized our schools without very much consideration for children as human beings—30-35 children for one
teacher, same grade level, same books, everyone must be quiet
in order to learn. Schools must change. The most important
characteristic of a school is the human element. Childhood is a
time of adventure and activity, and children need to be kept
active in school. The first responsibility of the teacher is to
establish good human relationships. Human development is
influenced by the affective domain just as it is by the cognitive.
The reciprocal relationship of affect and cognition requires that
learning tasks in school "turn kids on."

Although it is important to learn to live with other people, it
is imperative that each child learn to live with himself. Each
must learn to understand his assets and use them constructively.
He must discover his shortcomings and, if possible, improve on
them. He must develop a sense of self-protection that will
enable him to function at an efficient level.

Acquiring a knowledge of oneself is a continuous and
on-going experience. Successful living is not a thing but a
process: a continuous movement toward ever-changing values.
The primary function of the school program should be to
provide an environment that will enhance the development of
attitudes and values.

There should be many opportunities for a growing, responsible independence, with each child gradually accepting more
responsibility for his own learning and assuming greater
self-direction. Emphasis should be placed on the personal
development of the individual and on self-understanding.

The curriculum should not be a formal one that emphasizes
mastery of subject matter as an end in itself; rather, it should
emphasize the development of the child and take into consideration his interests, abilities and experiences. The subject matter

should be presented in such a way that it helps him grasp its functional value in relation to the problems of everyday living.

TEACHING FOR SELF-DIRECTION AND SELF-DISCIPLINE

A child's development of a positive self-concept, of attitudes and values, and of standards of behavior is influenced by the atmosphere and the environment in which he lives and learns. A well-developed human being is one who has self-respect, because this is a basic need of all humans, and a major task of the teacher in the open classroom is to help each child develop and maintain self-respect.

The activities of a child are directed toward satisfying his needs. His growth pattern affects his behavior and he has problems when he cannot satisfy his needs. In order to help each child find satisfaction in learning and develop self-confidence, teachers should plan a program to help children live a better and richer life in school.

The classroom environment is a great factor in the learning process, and the mental needs of a child cannot be met unless an intellectual environment is created in the classroom. The teacher should employ practices that encourage children to learn, and she can meet the physical needs of the children by providing a variety of activities to break up the monotony of long, quiet sitting periods. The emotional needs can be met by showing love for every child; therefore, the teacher should develop a personal relationship between every child and herself. To meet the social needs of the children, the teacher should provide democratic leadership and teach the children the democratic way of life. This would give each a sense of responsibility and help him fit into the group.

The teacher should strive to help each student to become self-disciplined, that is, to apply himself at all times to the best of his ability toward achieving his aims or goals. This type of discipline cannot be imposed on the individual; rather, it is the achievement of the individual himself. In teaching this type of discipline, the teacher should provide activities that are suitable to the child's interests and abilities. If he is interested in activity and if it is within his range of ability, he will want to discipline himself in order to get the most from the activity. This method of getting self-discipline also applies to group work. If individuals are interested in the activity and it is within their range of ability, the group will discipline itself so that each member may achieve the best possible results.

Long-range planning is an effective method by which teachers can organize their thinking in relation to the broad units of work to be considered. They should consider any purposes that the children might have and plan a program that will stimulate their interests and challenge their abilities.

Teachers should stimulate the interests of the children so that they begin to volunteer their ideas about what could be done in relation to the unit of work in question. The children can sit in an informal way with the teacher and talk about their purposes and goals, plan who is going to do what, form their committees, and get started. Then the teacher can work with each group to see that their group plans are workable and that everyone has been included in the activities of the group.

The teacher should also include in her plans a complete list of sources of a variety of materials that will be needed to fully develop every individual and group activity that is to be undertaken. There are basically two types of materials necessary: those used primarily to help the individual child, and those used to help a group of children understand important things that come up in group activities. In selecting this material the teacher should make certain that it will benefit those using it by helping them to grow. There must be consistency; there should not be excellent materials for use in teaching math and no art materials at all. There must be a balance of instructional materials selected to meet all the needs of the children and thus help them become well-rounded individuals.

Discussion experiences are necessary to give the children an opportunity to analyze their problems and decide what the group must do to solve them. Through discussion, each child gets an understanding of how everyone else in the group feels about the situation, and conclusions can be drawn about what they are going to do.

Teachers need to provide sharing experiences, which can be, for example, in the form of informal oral reporting. All the children of the group should be given an opportunity to present group ideas as well as individual ideas. A sharing experience should be a report of some type where every member of the group takes part in presenting to the others the results of the group work and activities.

During the group work all children should have some research experiences (See Figure 4-9). After the group has discovered what it is they need to know, they should use research materials and learn to think critically to sort out the important from the unimportant and thus be better prepared to report their findings.

Figure 4-9

Independent work experiences can be beneficial to those who complete their part of the group work first (See Figure 4-10). Independent work should be purposeful and functional and should contribute in some way to the work of the whole group. Some types of worthwhile independent work experiences are creative writing, creative art work, recreational reading, room and school duties such as student council reports,

Figure 4-10

practice on skills, working with concrete materials to help build concepts in arithmetic, or research reading. There are some kinds of independent work exercises that are best accomplished when given as homework assignments. Some of these might include simple scientific experiments, making collections, or locating pictures or magazine articles. Independent work, both at home and at school, is of little value unless it is shared with the group. Only through their contributions to the group can children develop a feeling of being a necessary part of that group.

A good program should definitely include evaluation experiences. Groups and individuals, when given frequent opportunities to look at their work and activities, can see how well they have accomplished their purposes and goals. Children should participate in the planning by helping set up the goals and objectives. When the interest of the group begins to lag, it becomes time for an evaluation period to see if the activities are of any value in helping to solve the problem. Children also benefit from the compliments and praise that come from the evaluation period. However, evaluation should not only be for praise, but also for discussion of questions such as, How could we do a better job next time?, What further steps can we take to solve this problem more completely?, What improvements can we make in our group process to best solve future problems?

The open classroom is enhanced by the encouragement of diversity. Because each child is unique and because his way of living is multi-directional, he needs to have a variety of educational experiences from which to choose. Through his selection he will have many opportunities to satisfy his many and various needs (See following illustration).

A child learns as he lives; thus, the most important kind of activity is the direct, first-hand experience—real experience from his environment. This kind of experience is relevant to the child because he has a particular need at this particular time.

Children need to have on-going experiences. Since no study is ever completely finished, provisions should be made to guide children in adding new meaning to a previously developed concept through the correlation of a new experience. And all learning grows out of experience. When a situation confronts a child, he draws from his background of experiences to help him solve the problem at hand. New ideas, skills and concepts, in order to be meaningful, must make sense to the child. In order to make sense there needs to be a correlation between the old and the new. In this way, the child learns as he lives.

A successful open classroom must also include experiences that help the child develop aesthetic values. He needs to have creative outlets in drama, singing, dancing, painting, drawing, writing, etc. In addition to these opportunities to express himself, he needs to share the creative works of his peers, his teachers, and the "masters." He needs to hear good music and to read good stories and poetry; he needs to see the great masterpieces of art.

Experiences in critical thinking are also a part of learning. Children need to examine many sources of information and tear ideas apart in order to learn to think critically before reaching conclusions. They need to question the answers, not answer the questions; they need to discover ideas, not cover content.

The various types of experiences suggested here need to be provided in a variety of situations. The child needs opportunities to be a member of a large group as well as small groups; he needs to work at times with children of his own age and at other times with children younger and/or older than he; he needs to work at times with children of the same sex and at other times with children of the opposite sex. The size of the group and the nature of those in the group with whom he works depend on his interest, ability, and the purpose of the activity. In addition to group work, the child should be given opportunities to work alone. The open classroom must provide for all these needs through various experiences in a variety of groupings.

TEACHER: AN EXPERT IN HUMAN RELATIONS

The learning activities of each child and the way he undertakes them enables the teacher to discover his difficulties, analyze his progress, and guide him in achieving desirable goals.

The free reading that a child does gives the teacher an opportunity to appraise his interests, likes and dislikes, and the deficiencies in his reading skills so that she can intelligently guide his future reading activities. Similarly, the child's performance in using numbers reveals his grasp of number concepts and mathematical processes. From his progress and achievement in the various areas of schoolwork, the teacher can discover where each pupil needs assistance.

In an open classroom the teacher must assume much responsibility in helping each child with problems such as building confidence in himself, developing greater independence in work and play, gaining better control of his emotions, and getting along better with his peers. To do this, the teacher must have faith in the children. Children are not born wicked, ill-mannered, and irritable; they are actually reflections of the adults they know, and their attitudes and behaviors are caused by the environment, which adults have created and to which children are expected to conform. Every delinquent is the result of the failure of many adults. It is important for the teacher to see each child as a unique human being, neither good nor bad except as his living makes him that way.

Typically, a teacher assumes her role to be only that of challenging each child to learn. This cannot be accomplished by simply presenting a group of skills and concepts and expecting the child to "learn" (See following illustration).

" I TEACH THOSE CHILDREN BUT THEY JUST DON'T LEARN!"

In an open classroom the teacher must recognize each child as a unique individual, different from all others. Each child needs to be considered differently; each needs to "do his own thing." The teacher should not expect children to conform to standardized procedures and graded materials; for there is no such thing as a standardized child.

Many schools have been treating growing human beings as clearly labeled packages to be run through the same assembly line for so long that the aggressions engendered during the school day are often manifested during after-school hours. For example, note the damage frequently done to school buildings during the night.

Children are not objects; they are human beings and should be treated as such. The teacher in an open classroom should be an adult who is interesting, understanding, sympathetic, and one to whom a child may relate confidently. The teacher should be a true friend of each child.

—SUMMARY—

The teacher is the most important single factor in the development of a school environment. Children look to the teacher as an example. They see how she lives more than they hear what she tells them to do. Openness must be the teacher's "style of living."

Children also look to teachers for guidance in the solution of their everyday problems; they expect teachers to be able to understand and help solve the problems of group living. That's what school is all about.

To the children, the teacher is an "expert" in human relations. The teacher should guide children in making decisions that will result in higher qualities of living and provide experiences that will lead to higher levels of thinking.

This "expert" should see her role as a resource person; she should provide guidance in group activities of planning, fulfilling and evaluating the total program; she should help children interpret the values and attitudes developed through "living" together in open classrooms.

chapter five | The Community and the Open Classroom

No educational program can hope to succeed unless it is believed in and supported by the citizens of the community. The citizens must fully understand the objectives toward which the teachers are striving, they must learn ways in which teachers are working with the pupils to reach stated objectives, and they must know the kinds of activities and experiences provided in open classrooms to achieve these purposes. What the school is trying to do and how it is attempting to do it must be understood by the community if the school is to gain its support.

COMMUNITY RELATIONS: TWO-WAY COMMUNICATION

The heart of the educational program includes a formulation of educational philosophy, a statement of objectives, a determination of the curriculum, and a development of the ways in which teachers and pupils work. The community should be involved in planning, operating, and evaluating the school program.

The most important function of educators is to establish two-way communication. The school program must be interpreted to the community so that people will better understand what is being taught, why it is taught, and how it is taught in open classrooms. Members of the community must offer ideas and suggestions in order for the educational program to really meet the needs of the community. Community involvement in education fosters the development of individual human dignity and self-realization. Both meaning and vitality will be added to the program of education when the school and the community are bound together by common purpose.

Community Involvement

With emphasis upon human relations, personal contacts and the cooperation of all concerned, the school becomes a place of interaction. The diagram in Figure 5-1 illustrates that input comes from those groups interacting with each other as well as providing services to the school.

The interaction school becomes a place where ideas are born, where people are respected as human beings, where pre-service and in-service teachers learn and practice the skills of teaching toward the goal of providing for the needs of people to learn and grow.

Ultimate goals of community involvement include:

1. the evolution of an interaction school;
2. the realization of a philosophy that education is a "live-in";
3. the interaction school becoming the center of community life;

4. improved community-school-university relations;
5. a relevant teacher-education program for preparing teachers for open classrooms.

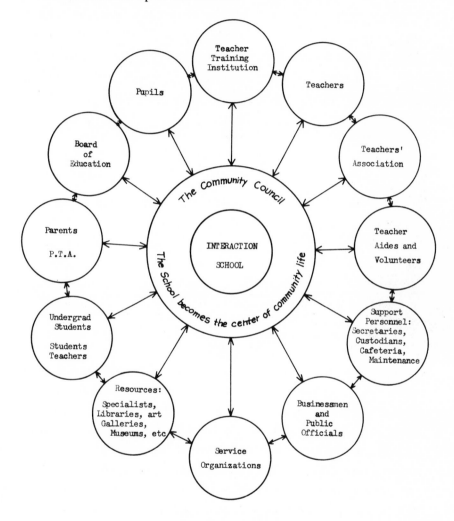

"EDUCATION IS A LIVE-IN"

Figure 5-1

Utilizing Human Resources: Everyone Is a Teacher

One does not need a teaching certificate in order to teach; for most human learning is not the result of instruction, but of the interrelationships of human beings as they develop in social situations. Regardless of background or training, each human has something to give to others. An open classroom is a social situation in which people can interact in a variety of groups and in various ways. This interaction is teaching; people learn from each other.

In an open classroom, where each child is being instructed on his own achievement level, teacher aides and volunteers help teachers individualize instruction and help fulfill the goals established for the program. The more adults sharing the work load the more successful the program can be in meeting the unique needs of individuals. By using these auxiliary personnel we are able to free the teachers of many time-consuming tasks and clerical jobs and, thus, provide them with more opportunities for individualizing instruction.

Although aides are paid and volunteers are not, both may perform the same tasks. However, since the volunteer is not paid, she is not required to accept the obligations and discipline that are required of aides or teachers. Some of the duties of aides and volunteers are: taking attendance and keeping routine records; collecting funds for various purposes and keeping accounts; correcting objective tests and making up lists and charts for the teachers; supervising playground activities; supervising the lunchroom; helping younger children with their clothing; supervising lavatory periods; checking out library books; caring for and operating audio-visual equipment; typing and duplicating; answering the telephone; running errands to the office; filing work in children's folders; making arrangements for field trips; assisting children in construction of bulletin boards; supervising quiet activities and rest periods; listening to and sharing thoughts as they are dictated by the children; above all, interacting with the children.

Although many of these tasks are closely related to the teaching function, aides and volunteers are not replacing the teacher. A teacher has the responsibility of analyzing the instructional needs of her students, of prescribing the course of study that will best meet those needs, and of utilizing the resources of an aide or volunteer in helping to carry out her plans.

In short, the philosophy of the use of an aide or volunteer should be that her activities be restricted only by her own personal limitations in any duty that the regular classroom teachers assign to her. By freeing teachers from such work we enable the professional staff to use that time to plan and prepare their classroom work and coach individual children. The teachers feel better about their profession, their status is raised in the eyes of parents and pupils, and they have an opportunity for an occasional break. Therefore, their attitudes and morale are better and they have more energy for classroom work.

In an open classroom where each child is being instructed on his own achievement level, the clerical aides help teachers individualize instruction by preparing all kinds of drills and practice exercises on different levels of difficulty. These are given to individual children according to their achievement levels. This enables pupils to work independently while the teacher circulates throughout the room giving individual help, or calling together small groups for further instruction. Thus, while most of the students are working independently, the teacher has time to confer with individuals who are having difficulty as well as those working on special projects and depth studies.

The presence of other adults in the classroom also serves to encourage teachers to examine their own attitudes, personality traits, and classroom standards and procedures. Many teachers are now making more detailed and better plans because they have help in providing and carrying out more worthwhile learning activities for individual children.

A properly trained aide or volunteer is able to perform limited instructional tasks under the general guidance and supervision of a classroom teacher. Since we believe that the primary purpose of teacher aides is to increase the effectiveness of the teacher, it therefore seems logical that aides should help carry out teacher-made plans for large- and small-group instruction.

Certainly a teacher aide can read a story to a group of children, repeat teacher directions, help a child locate information in the materials center, listen to a child read orally, or even help several children in drill exercises.

On-the-job training by the staff is the best method of getting help from aides and volunteers. An orientation program should be planned to explain what the aides can do and how instruction can be improved by using aides. Explore the various abilities and skills of the aides; teach them how to use the office machines, files, and audio-visual equipment and materials; assign them to suitable work; supervise and evaluate their work; ask them for suggestions and self-evaluation.

Aides can be trained to work with individuals, to write experience stories with small groups, and to continue phonics drills on a one-to-one basis. One-to-one mathematics drills can also be successfully conducted by some aides.

Using plans made by teachers, aides and volunteers can help children who have been absent with back assignments. Also, they can see that pre-assigned work is carried out and assist individuals who are having difficulty.

The use of teacher aides and volunteers is closely tied to individualization of instruction. Because of the variety of talent and ability, the best utilization of aides can be achieved by pooling their time rather than assigning them to a specific teacher all day.

Teachers should request an aide for a particular time for a particular job. From these requests a weekly schedule can be set up. Some aide time should be unscheduled to provide flexibility so that a teacher could request additional help for an extra task not included on the schedule. This might be a one-to-one task. After all these requests are summarized, a weekly schedule can be made for volunteers and aides.

For example: Teacher X requested an aide to type experience stories from 9:00 A.M. to 10:15 A.M. on Monday, Wednesday, and Friday, and an aide to help get the children washed and ready for lunch each day. In order to honor these requests, each Monday, Wednesday, and Friday, an aide who types is assigned to this teacher from 9:00 to 10:15 A.M. Another aide, one who does not type, is assigned every day at 11:00 A.M. to help the children wash up for lunch.

As an example of an aide's day, Mrs. E. spends from 9:00 A.M. to 10:15 A.M. in room 22 typing experience stories as they are dictated by individual children. At 10:15 she goes outside for playground duty during the morning recess. After a short break she goes to room 4 where she assists the teacher by checking arithmetic papers and helping children with assigned individual work. At 11:45 she goes to the cafeteria for lunchroom duty. Since she is unscheduled for the afternoon, she goes to the office to type and duplicate classroom work for teachers. Occasionally she is assigned to a class for a special project or as extra help for a teacher not scheduled to have aide assistance at that time.

Through this type of scheduling the teachers know which

aide they will have on which day, at what time, and for what task. They also know that they can get additional help by requesting it through the office. By pooling aide time in this manner you will get the most help from teacher aides and volunteers.

Figure 5-2 is a sample of a letter that could be used in soliciting volunteer aides. In addition to parent volunteers, many high school and middle school students are very much interested in assisting elementary children. Students often make excellent aides.

Dear Parents and Friends:

This is a follow-up of the P.T.A. meeting on the 22nd in reference to volunteer aides. We need you.

Some of the duties of volunteers might include taking attendance and keeping routine records, collecting funds for various purposes, working in the health room, correcting objective tests and making up lists and charts for the teacher, supervising playground activities, supervising the lunchroom, helping younger children with their clothing, checking out library books, caring for and operating audio-visual equipment, typing and duplicating, answering the telephone, filing work in children's folders, making arrangements for field trips, assisting children in construction of bulletin boards, supervising quiet activities and rest periods, and listening to and sharing thoughts as they are dictated by children, etc.

Although many of these tasks are closely related to the teaching function, aides will *not* replace the teacher. A teacher has the responsibility of analyzing the instructional needs of her students, of prescribing the course of study that will best meet those needs, and of utilizing the resources of an aide in helping to carry out her plans.

I am planning to conduct two workshops for parent volunteers during the summer. The sessions will be at the school from 9-11:30 a.m. on July 12 and August 9. You are invited to attend either of these sessions.

If you would like to volunteer to help as an aide next year, please complete the form below and return it to school by June 9th. If you would like additional information, please contact me.

Sincerely,

Lee L. Smith
Principal

_____

————————I would like to be a volunteer aide next year.
————————I would like to attend the parent workshop on July 12.
————————I would like to attend the parent workshop on August 9.
————————I will not be able to attend either workshop, but would like to be a volunteer aide next year.

Name_____

Address_____

Phone_____

Figure 5-2

The behavior of a child at any age is strongly influenced by the opinions of his peers. Under the guidance of the teacher, children can enter constructively into the instructional phase of school life.

Peer teaching can be done successfully in several ways. Perhaps the easiest way is on a one-to-one basis. This works well in drill work where both need to practice the same thing, for instance, some division facts. In this way, pupils could take turns in checking each other's work.

One-to-one situations are limitless. Another example might be one child listening to another give his campaign speech, which he has prepared for the student body in seeking the office of president of student council.

A teacher can divide his room into many small groups (two to three children) and have peer teachers from other rooms come in to give specific instruction. The teacher can plan all the details with the peer teachers or simply give them the task and leave the selection of materials and methods to the students. This is a highly successful technique because children speak each other's language and can often explain something to peers much easier than adults can. In another situation a child who is very good at oral reading might spend a few minutes reading orally to a peer group of less mature readers.

Experience has proved that, many times, the peer teacher is learning as much if not more than those being taught. It should be pointed out also that a peer teacher is continuing to develop a positive self-concept as he participates in this leadership role. In these experiences children are learning as they live and work together and become more and more concerned with the "human" characteristic of their school.

AN OPEN COMMUNITY:
"New Town," Columbia, Maryland[1]

The community is the setting in which the child lives and learns, in which he develops meanings and concepts essential to an understanding of group living. In this setting he experiences life in a democracy. Experiences in church, stores, theaters, home, neighborhood and school become his background of meanings for study, thought and expression. The community is the child's laboratory for learning about man's way of living.

The community also provides first-hand experiences in the social functions of group living. Some of the richest instructional resources are found in the immediate neighborhood: field

---

[1]Information about Columbia was taken from *Visitor's Guide to Columbia,* a publication of Howard Research and Development Corporation, November 1971. Used by permission.

trips, interesting people, radio interviews, etc. Children can cooperate in local projects and become participants in community activities. The child's own daily experiences in the community are a great source of learning in the open classroom.

Columbia, Maryland is people-centered. It is being built on the idea that a city can be an efficient and comfortable place for living and working, and that only a city can provide the full range of services, institutions, recreational and cultural attractions that a family needs for its growth.

Columbia is soon to be a complete city, not another random extension of the American suburbs. The new city will be the focal point of activity—retail, commercial, business, industrial and recreational—for the corridor between Washington and Baltimore. This is one of the most rapidly growing areas in the nation today, each year seeing almost 100,000 people move into new homes and jobs.

When the city is completed, there will be 110,000 residents living in seven villages around a central downtown area. Columbia is being developed by the Rouse Company in a joint venture with the Connecticut General Life Insurance Company. The city is being built entirely by private enterprise, which will have made an investment of about $2 billion by the time of completion.

The Columbia plan starts with a neighborhood of 2,000 to 5,000 people. Near the center of each neighborhood is an elementary school, park and playground, swimming pool, small community building and convenience store. From two to four neighborhoods make up a village of from 10,000 to 15,000 people. Each village center provides the kinds of shopping and services a family needs frequently, such as a bank, supermarket, pharmacy, barber shop, beauty salon, laundry, and professional offices. Most village centers will have middle and high schools, along with village-wide religious and recreational facilities.

Columbia's downtown is just beginning to grow. It starts with a 32-acre lake and extends westward. Along the lake are the Exhibit Center, five office buildings and the Cross Keys Inn, with 150 rooms and a lounge. The Mall in Columbia is the commercial heart of downtown, featuring two large department stores and 102 specialty shops and services. Shoppers peruse the Mall completely protected from the elements: inside, it's springtime the year round. Glass pyramids atop the mall and skylights topping most walk areas allow natural light to filter through, casting attractive patterns on the brick ground level and carpeted top level.

Beneath the pyramids are tropical gardens, courtyards, pools and fountains, one of which shoots water 25 feet into the air. Shoppers can rest or have a snack while watching the passing scene in a park-like atmosphere. Eventually, plans call for the mall to have five department stores and some 300 shops and services.

Nearby the mall is Symphony Woods, the 40-acre, permanent downtown park. The Merriweather Post Pavilion of Music, which can accommodate 10,000 people is also located there. Nearby is the Garland Dinner Theatre.

The Columbia plan has designated more than 20 per cent of the acreage for permanent open spaces, including woods, streams, lakes, golf courses, pathways and school playgrounds interwoven throughout the city. Another 20 per cent of the land is set aside for the business and industry necessary for the growth and balance of the new city and its institutions. The plan's intent is to keep full city facilities proportionate to the number of people in order to enhance rather than detract from the quality of life. The city's goals include respect for the land's natural beauty and opportunity for growth and life.

Be it a single-family house, townhouse, midrise or garden apartment, Columbia offers housing to suit most family sizes and tastes, and building styles range from colonial to contemporary. There is something to interest people of all ages in the city: parks, swimming pools, lakes, tennis courts, bike and walking paths, two golf courses, a horse center and a state-regulated game preserve. Recreational activities for young people have been organized through the village and neighborhood centers, and the Columbia Association's recreation programs include sports, music, drama, nature, hobbies, dance, social activities, day camps and adult athletic leagues. Sailboats, rowboats, paddleboats and canoes may be rented on the downtown lake from May through October, and fishing goes on most of the year. In winter, when the lakes freeze, skaters take over. A family can swim year round at the Columbia Swim Center, or in the summer at the neighborhood pools. Tennis courts are available in each village. The Columbia Tennis Barn offers indoor tennis from October through April.

River Hill Farm, a 450-acre state-regulated game preserve, provides local hunting grounds for chukar partridge, pheasant and quail from October through March. The Columbia Health Club is open year round and offers steam baths, saunas, exercise rooms, whirlpools, massages, and facilities for squash and handball. The Columbia Ice Rink operates nine months a year, from early fall through late spring; the Columbia Horse Center offers equestrian instruction and schedules horse shows throughout the year.

Residents have formed more than 100 organizations, ranging from partisan politics to crewel work groups. Teen centers are located in each of the village centers; activities include dances, rap sessions, parties, athletic leagues and informal gatherings. Civic groups periodically sponsor special events such as film series, choral concerts, plays and community dances. Columbia's birthday in June and the Fourth of July are festive occasions in the city.

Starting at the nursery level, Columbia offers schooling for children through college age. In addition, many public service courses, as well as college credit courses, are available to the community.

Pre-schoolers can head for several nursery school programs starting at three years of age. Day-care programs for children of working mothers and hourly day-care programs are available. Cooperative nursery schools organized by parents are widely used, and a Montessori program is also in operation. The Singer Learning Center is a privately operated school with innovative pre-school and day-care programs for children of ages three through eight.

Public schools in Columbia are operated by the Howard County Department of Education under a K-5 elementary, 6-8 middle, and 9-12 high school plan, featuring "open space" classrooms, team teaching, nongrading and other variations from the traditional approaches to public education.

Columbia's plans call for over 20 elementary schools, one to be conveniently located in each neighborhood. Land is set aside in each village for middle and high schools to be built at the option of the Howard County Board of Education.

Howard Community College is located on a 110-acre campus and offers a transfer program paralleling the first two years of a four-year college and enabling students to continue studies toward bachelor degrees. Technical and vocational courses, aiming at associate degrees and diplomas, are also offered as are numerous non-credit courses in service to the community.

Columbia's goal for business and industrial development is to provide jobs for 65,000 people by the time the city is complete. About 3,000 acres of land are designated exclusively for business and industrial use. Over 65 industries have already located in Columbia. These firms represent many kinds of industry, including distributing, light manufacturing and research and development.

Catholics, Jews and Protestants share common facilities in the Interfaith Center. Facilities include offices, conference spaces and areas for religious services. Programs for religious education, family life and counseling services and pastors' counseling are regularly available at the Center. Community groups and county agencies also meet in the multi-purpose areas of the facility, and shoppers are encouraged to stop in for coffee at the Interfaith Center lounge. Regular art shows are featured there also. The Columbia Cooperative Ministry has been established as a joint venture to examine new opportunities for mission and service by the church in an urban environment.

The Columbia Medical Plan is a prepaid, group practice health care program provided by the Columbia Hospital and Clinics Foundation in affiliation with the Johns Hopkins Medical Institution. Membership is open to all Columbia residents and to residents of Howard County whose employers offer the plan as a fringe benefit.

The Columbia Park and Recreation Association, referred to as C.A., is a private, non-profit corporation supported by all Columbia property owners—residential, business and commercial. The corporation was formed to build and operate a broad range of property and facilities beneficial to the life and well-being of people living and working in Columbia. C.A. builds, operates and maintains community facilities such as parks, playgrounds, swimming pools, golf courses, meeting rooms, nursery schools, public transportation and, with the residents, develops and operates programs in the community.

To finance C.A., owners of all taxable property pay an annual charge. Some C.A. facilities are free and open to the public. Fees are charged at others to help offset operating costs. Resident Columbians, because they must pay the annual charge, receive sizable discounts for use of facilities charging fees.

Columbia residents—property owners and renters—have a voice in community affairs through their respective village associations. Each village association meets monthly to conduct activities determined by annually elected representatives. Columbia is an unincorporated town governed by Howard County, and the county's charter form of government provides for a full-time county executive and five councilmen, all elected at large to four-year terms. Howard County provides Columbia with such services as education, fire and police protection, sanitation, sewers and water.

James W. Rouse, president of the Rouse Company and "father of Columbia," once said that "Columbia should be a garden in which people can grow." Mr. Rouse, in a statement before a committee of Congress in support of the New Communities Section, Title II of the Housing Bill for 1966, summarized his philosophy on the humanistic development for the new town. He said,

> Our cities grow by accident, by whim of the private developer and public agencies. . . .By this irrational process, non-communities are born—formless places, without order, beauty or reason, with no visible respect for people or the land. . . .The vast, formless spread of housing, pierced by the unrelated spotting of schools, churches, stores, creates areas so huge and irrational that they are out of scale with people—beyond their grasp and comprehension—too big for people to feel a part of, responsible for, important in. . . .
>
> I believe that the ultimate test of civilization is whether or not it contributes to the growth and improvement of mankind. Does it

uplift, inspire, stimulate, and develop the best in man? There really can be no other right purpose of community except to provide an environment and an opportunity to develop better people. The most successful community would be that which contributed the most by its physical form, its institutions, and its operation to the growth of people.[2]

The number-one goal, to create a social and physical environment that would work for people and that would nourish human growth, is a reality. Columbia is truly an "open classroom."

COMMUNITY SCHOOL

A community school project returns us to the awareness of the fact that education is a total community activity. Thus, the formation of intellectual and social habits of worth are learned not solely in the school. By the school and the community interacting, the school can play an important role in the formation of student values and lifestyles. The community is an open classroom.

There should be no sharp dichotomy between school activities and community programs. Although the principal should remain the educational leader of all activities, there should be a coordinator of the activities of the community component. He should report to the principal all community participation activities proposed and develop with the principal the implementation of these activities.

The mechanism for community participation in decision-making should be an advisory council, and the council should

---

[2] James W. Rouse, President, The Rouse Company, Columbia, Maryland. Used by permission.

be open to all interested members of the community who are at least ten years old. The council should serve in an advisory capacity to:

1. suggest policy and budgetary decisions;
2. determine the needs of the community;
3. operate community school programs;
4. relate community activities to the nature of education;
5. act as a resource to the school.

A community school project is an attempt to infuse an authentic community life into a building that was heretofore darkened and locked during after-school hours. However, if a school is a totalitarian state during school hours and attempts through some magical transformation to become a place of fun and freedom in the evening programs, the inconsistency is certain to weaken the program. A community school program is intended specifically to be a natural extension of the school day. An open classroom is a place where one has opportunity to continue his own style of living.

What makes a community school project genuinely unique is something more than the fact that we ask people to make the school a viable, pulsating part of their community lives. We should ask that it be an active element in the family structure. There have been many theoretical pronouncements of this sort without an accompanying program. The composite programs, highly organized and structured, have exhibited every virtue except life. Rather than plan a program for the members of the community and say to them, "These are the activities we have planned for you; come and take advantage of them," we should involve them and have them plan their own activities.

The interest centers should be open and should contain

interesting activities, but a person should not have to enroll or register; he should be free to come and go as he desires. If this project is to be for the community, then it must be responsive to the community's experience. The school must become a live, breathing part of the community so that the community becomes a much better place in which to live. This is the philosophy of the open classroom.

OPEN CLASSROOMS AT THE UNIVERSITY: TEACHER TRAINING

In order to prepare teachers for open classrooms there must be a change in programs of teacher education. Colleges and universities must themselves establish open classrooms. Prospective teachers need to be in schools and with children; they cannot become good teachers for open classrooms by being boxed in a university classroom to "hear" how to teach.

Learning is a process that occurs within the learner. One learns according to personal history, aspirations and interests, in addition to the external characteristics of the learning situation. Because learning is an individual experience, the learning situation should be structured so that each student can approach the task to be mastered in a way that is uniquely his. The prospective teacher must be actively involved in the learning situation, continually interacting with it and thus changing his perceptions of both the situation and himself. The feeling of and the desire for mastery are potent driving forces in the learning situation. The outcome of instruction is a new level of mastery: the learner should be able to do something he could not do before exposure to the learning situation.

The setting in which teacher education occurs cannot be

separated from the instructional program. A school building can affect an instructional program by impeding it, facilitating it, or being neutral. Open classrooms are designed to be neutral so that they can be molded by the users to meet their own unique needs. Open classrooms encourage movement, exploration, discovery, interaction and cooperation among both students and teachers. Although prospective teachers can be taught in groups, they learn as individuals; they learn at differenct rates, with different styles, and in response to different stimuli. An individualized instructional plan is designed to provide learning materials of varying levels of difficulty presented in a variety of ways. The role of a professor in an individualized program is to diagnose the learning and personal characteristics of each student and to select appropriate educational activities to meet specific behavioral objectives.

Teacher educators must view the open classroom as a philosophy of education and develop a commitment to the philosophy in planning their programs.

There must be provision for individualized instruction to meet the unique needs of prospective teachers. Individualized instruction must be viewed as a process by which each learner is assisted in developing his own unique style. The process may vary not only in rate, but in approach and content as well.

The development of human relations skills must also become a major concern. Performance objectives should be utilized as the basis of the program to permit prospective teachers to demonstrate competency in teaching prior to certification. Flexibility built into the training sequences will afford alternative methods of realizing objectives.

Teacher educators should encourage each prospective teacher to develop a positive self-concept and his own teaching style with self-direction and self-evaluation as integral parts. Modern technology should be utilized to assist students in developing their teaching techniques and in evaluating their own progress and a variety of field experiences should be provided early in the program and continued throughout the training period to permit trainees to try out their style of teaching. Teacher preparation should be viewed as a continuous, lifelong process rather than a program that ends with graduation.

There needs to be a greater cooperation among open schools, open communities and open universities so that in-service can become an integral part of this continuous training. Just as the schools can be used for settings of practical experiences for the student teacher, the regular teachers can utilize the resources of the university to upgrade their teaching techniques and methods for creating and operating open classrooms.

—SUMMARY—

The heart of the educational program includes a formulation of the educational philosophy, a statement of objectives, a determination of the curriculum, and a development of the ways in which teachers and pupils work. The community should be involved in planning, operating, and evaluating the school program.

The most important function of educators is to establish two-way communication. The school program must be interpreted to the community so that people will better understand what is being taught, why it is taught, and how it is taught in open classrooms. The community must offer ideas and suggestions in order for the educational program to really meet the needs of the community.

With emphasis upon human relations, personal contacts, and

the cooperation of all concerned, the school becomes a place of interaction. The interaction school becomes a place where ideas are born, where people are respected as human beings, where pre-service and in-service teachers learn and practice the skills of teaching toward the goal of determining and providing for the needs of people to learn and grow.

Regardless of background or training, each human has something to give others. An open classroom is a social situation in which people can interact in a variety of groups and in various ways. This interaction is teaching. People learn from each other.

In an open classroom teacher aides and volunteers help teachers individualize instruction and help fulfill the goals established for the program. In addition to parent volunteers, many high school and middle school students can make excellent contributions as aides in an elementary school.

The behavior of a child at any age is strongly influenced by the opinions of his peers. Under the guidance of the teacher, children can enter constructively into the instructional phase of school life.

Experience has proved that, many times, the peer teacher is learning as much if not more than those being taught. It should be pointed out also that a peer teacher is continuing to develop a positive self-concept as he participates in this leadership role. In these experiences children are learning as they live and work together and become more concerned for the "human" characteristic of their school.

The community is the setting in which the child lives and learns, in which he develops meanings and concepts essential to an understanding of group living. In this setting he experiences life in a democracy. The community is the child's laboratory for learning about man's way of living. The child's own daily experiences in the community are a resource that can enrich learning in the open classroom.

Columbia, Maryland is an example of an open community. It is being built on the idea that a city can be an efficient and comfortable place for living and working, and that only a city can provide the full range of services, institutions, recreation and cultural attractions that a family needs for its growth. This "new town" is people-centered; it is truly an "open classroom."

A community school project returns us to the awareness of the fact that education is a total community activity. The formation of intellectual and social habits of worth are not only learned in the school. By the school and the community interacting, the school can play an important role in the formation of student values and lifestyles.

In order to prepare teachers for open classrooms there must be a change in programs of teacher education. Colleges and universities must establish open classrooms. Prospective teachers need to be in schools and with children; they cannot become good teachers for open classrooms by being boxed in a university classroom to "hear" how to teach. An open classroom is a "doing" place. It involves all facets of the community.

chapter six | Nongradedness and the Open Classroom

The nongraded school represents an endeavor to facilitate through organization a plan for the continuous growth of the child. The nongraded school organization is a vertical one, which provides for differentiated rates and means of progression toward achievement of educational goals.

As stated earlier, the basic tenet of the philosophy of the open classroom is that education is a live-in. Each person is uniquely different. Meeting individual differences is not a technique; it is a way of living. It includes accepting others, respecting their contributions, working for the kind of group operation in which each individual knows he has a part, and encouraging each to give his best in each situation.

Since nongradedness is concerned with meeting individual needs, it has become a vehicle for creating open classrooms.

DEFINITION OF NONGRADEDNESS

Nongradedness is a philosophy of education which makes

possible the adjusting of teaching and administrative procedures to meet the different social, mental, and physical capacities among children. It uses an organizational plan that eliminates grade labels, promotes flexible grouping and continuous progress, and permits the utilization of meaningful individualized instruction.

PHILOSOPHY OF NONGRADEDNESS

Nongrading is a way of life. The philosophy of nongradedness is known by many names, with the emphasis on the plan and the years covered reflected in the name. Some of the names mentioned in the literature are: nongraded primary; primary unit; continuous progress; primary cycle; levels system; flexible primary unit; primary block; and nongraded school. (Although some use the term ungraded, most systems prefer nongraded.)

A nongraded school organization recognizes the variability among students in all aspects of their development. This type of school organization provides for differentiated rates and means of progression toward the achievement of educational goals.

The primary function of the nongraded school program is to provide an environment that will enhance the development of values and attitudes. There should be many opportunities for a growing, responsible independence, with each child gradually accepting more responsibility for his own learning and assuming greater self-direction. Emphasis should be placed on the personal development of the individual and on self-understanding.

The curriculum should not be a formal one that emphasizes mastery of subject matter as an end in itself, but rather it should emphasize the development of the child and take into consideration his interests, abilities, and experiences. The subject matter should be presented in such a way that it helps him grasp its functional value in relation to the problems of everyday living.

GUIDELINES FOR GROUPING IN NONGRADED SCHOOLS

The nongraded school organization must be geared to the individual, moving at his own rate and in his own way through a continuous program of instruction. During the process of classifying pupils into instructional groups the following guidelines should be considered:

- The grouping should provide for individual differences.
- The size of the classroom group should be reasonable and flexible.
- The structure should encourage desirable interaction among the children.
- The grouping should permit cooperative teacher-pupil planning.
- The grouping should serve to encourage selection of subject matter to meet individual needs.
- The grouping should encourage the use of a variety of approaches to learning.
- The grouping should make it possible for teachers to study each child, analyze his specific needs, and prescribe appropriate instructional activities.
- The grouping should create a relaxed atmosphere for the teachers; it should free them from having to achieve predetermined, unrealistic standards and goals.
- The grouping should encourage a creative atmosphere for children, free from unreasonable requirements not justified by their maturity level.

CHANGING TO A NONGRADED PROGRAM

It seems that we really face a challenge to provide our children with something that will help them live in the environment that we have created for them. Our society has created a complicated world, and our children have to have something meaningful to get them through it. We should accept this challenge of providing educational experiences that will help them learn how to live, how to survive and, perhaps, how to contribute toward the improvement of the environment we have created.

We have been working too long in a lock-step fashion. We need more creativity. We need to capitalize on the diversity of children. Occasionally, we need to get out of their way, at least for a few minutes.

Our children are not achieving as they should. You know it; I know it; and what are we doing about it? We need to teach more for critical thinking and solving of real problems, not problems that we make up, but problems concerned with how they are going to live—things that are real to them. Every teacher must be, in a certain sense, a guidance counselor. Children should be able to look to the teacher as the expert in human relations, the expert in solving real problems.

Grouping is very important, and there are many ways it can be done. The best way for you is the way that will meet the needs of your children and your community. Grouping can be done in a self-contained situation, and it can be done also in team situations. It can be done homogeneously; it can be done heterogeneously. The best way for you is the way that will best meet the needs of the children in your shcool, taking into consideration your staff.

I think the most important point to make about grouping is that it must be flexible. Don't have a group situation set up in

September for the entire year. You might need to change it tomorrow.

Children are the most important ingredient of change. That's really the purpose of school. You've heard conflict between child-centered and subject-centered curricula. A child is a human being and, therefore, the curriculum must be child-centered. I don't mean what was done in the name of Progressive Education a few years back. It failed because it was misinterpreted. "Good morning, boys and girls. What do you want to do today?" or "Good morning, teacher. Do I have to do what I want to again today?" By child-centered education I mean treating children as human beings and meeting their needs. Each child is unique. He has unique needs, and therefore the curriculum must be planned to meet the child's needs. It has to be child-centered, not subject-centered. But you don't throw the subject matter out. You are going to teach him something. You have to teach him what he needs when he needs it.

What about personnel—the staff involved? It's not just teachers; it's not just principals. It includes these people, but it also includes other children as peer teachers. It includes custodians, cafeteria personnel, secretaries, parents, and the community. All must be involved. It is easier for you to make a change if all are involved from the planning stages on. Occasionally, some of us go through the back door. We become involved first; then we have people annoyed with us, and we have to do something about getting everybody into the act. You can accomplish the job alone, but it is best to have all of your helpers involved so that everybody can assist with the planning. Then, if it goes wrong, part of the blame lies with them.

Attitudes imply values. If we can, through our example and our program, teach children to develop a favorable attitude toward school and develop a kindly feeling for each other, we are giving them something that will be with them long after they forget many of the other concepts we tried to teach them. "We are in this thing together. This is our school; we are all a part of it. This is what we want to do; this is why we want to do it. I am not going to throw a stone because it might hit one of my buddies and hurt him." Concern for our school; concern for each other. Here the concept of happiness enters. If children are happy about school, and their attitude is that school is a good place, that's your best report card. School should not be a place in which children experience pain for five or six hours, then go somewhere to find pleasure. Rather, school should be a continuation of a way of life. School should be a "caring" place.

Enthusiasm is the key to the success of any program. All involved in the program must be enthusiastic for change, or it is not going to work. If nongradedness is your way of life, then smile and be enthusiastic about it.

What recommendations do I offer for changing to a non-graded program? First, I suggest that you plan to reorganize the entire school at the same time. It doesn't seem sensible to have a nongraded primary, and then at the beginning of the fourth year in school to return to traditional grade levels. Nor does it seem logical to have a nongraded intermediate program for children who have had their first three years of school experience in a graded program. In fact, it would seem that students at all levels of education should be able to take the courses they really need, omit those that are not practical for them, and move through these courses at their own rate and in their own way.

Second, in initiating a nongraded program, you should plan a full program of orientation for the entire community. Include the children, the parents, the Board of Education, the Super-intendent or the Director of Education and the entire staff, including the secretary and the custodians.

The third recommendation is that you develop the attitude that nongrading is a philosophy based on the continuous progress of each child. You need to develop a program that will meet the specific needs of your community. You have to get your staff together and say, "What is it that we want our children to be like when they have completed our program? After we have established these goals, how are we going to accomplish this? How can we do it within the limitations set up for us?"

Next, develop the concept of flexibility in your school organization and scheduling. The latter is especially important. You've heard high school principals talk about the difficult job of setting up the master schedule each spring. Once it's set up, it's established for the year. "That student can't have this, because the section is filled." "If so-and-so doesn't take that when I have him scheduled, he can't take it at all this year." Don't put Jack in that box.

The next recommendation is that you plan to utilize fully all the help you can get, including teacher aides, if you have the money. If you haven't the money, use parent volunteers, and regardless of whether you have money or not, use peer teachers. For instance, while a student runs a projector, the teacher can be working with individuals. Following this same line of thought, plan to use some form of team teaching. Call it cooperative teaching, if you will. Have teachers working together on problems. Utilize, whenever possible, resource people, such as special teachers, psychologists, speech therapists, music teachers, art teachers, etc.

If you are going to plan for continuous progress, you must also plan for continuous evaluation. You must keep accurate records on students so that you know where each one is. It will be necessary to modify your system of reporting to parents. The best report card is a happy child. The next best method of reporting is through conferences, and another approach is the written conference—a narrative report.

I have suggested that you not try to "cram the child full of facts," but rather teach him how to think. Teach him how to use the resources of the school. Teach him how to be creative, how to work on problem solving. Don't worry about facts, so long as he knows how to find them when he needs them, and how to think through and solve his own problems.

So far as you are concerned, I would suggest, again, that you have enthusiasm. If you are going to make a change to nongradedness, then be enthusiastic about it. The important thing about getting somewhere is starting where you are. Start where you are and move ahead as you are ready. I can't tell you where. There is no one way. My way may not work for you. The only thing that will work is the philosophy of nongradedness: using common sense in treating everyone as a human being.

IMPLEMENTING THE NONGRADED PHILOSOPHY

On the following pages are brief descriptions of several nongraded schools. Each program has been developed by people starting where they were and planning a program to meet their needs.

A Nongraded Elementary School

"The Walls Came Tumblin' Down" is the title of a slide presentation which shows successes of the staff of South Frederick Elementary School in Frederick, Maryland as they were "tearing down the walls" of the entire graded school organization, grades 1 to 6, at the same time.

The first and most obvious wall to crumble was that of the

grade barrier. The idea of grades has become so ingrained in educational thinking that even textbooks have been rigidly prescribed by grade level. Each child has been expected to come up to the same standard by the end of the year regardless of his ability and interest.

The nongraded plan at South Frederick provides an alternative to the pass or fail dilemma. In the graded school, the child who gets off to a slow start presents a particular problem in June. Shall he be passed to a grade for which he is not ready, or failed and required to repeat the many things he has done successfully? Under the continuous program he merely picks up in September where he left off in June. In the nongraded school he will proceed from level to level at his own pace.

Also to crumble were the walls of the self-contained classroom (recently termed "self-contaminated"). This is the traditional form of classroom organization where one teacher is left alone, behind closed doors, to teach 30 to 35 children the prescribed curriculum for a given grade in ten months.

The organizational patterns of nongradedness and team teaching are flexible arrangements that promote the philosophy of continuous growth and permit the utilization of meaningful individualized instruction.

Changing to a nongraded program is a two-phased operation. The nongraded school is an organizational plan—a different way of grouping in which the grouping is very flexible. The continuous movement of children according to their own rate of maturation is an administrative tool to encourage and promote the philosophy of continuous growth. Instruction must be geared to meet the needs of each child and must be individualized as much as possible.

In this plan there are no grades 1, 2, 3, 4, 5, or 6. The program is organized in a series of levels in the skill areas of

Language Arts and Mathematics. Recognizing that all pupils will not necessarily perform equally well in all areas, a child may operate at one particular level in reading, while operating at another level in mathematics. Each child is placed in an instructional group in which it is felt he can make the best progress from level to level at his own rate. The grouping is very flexible and is changed whenever a need arises. The program emphasizes the importance of and helps bring about a greater recognition of individual differences in children. Continuous evaluation of each child is made so that his needs may be analyzed, learning activities may be prescribed, and the proper materials may be provided to help the learner develop to his fullest potential. When pupils are allowed to progress through the school at their own individual rates, the barrier to learning caused by the fear of failure is eliminated.

Because children are regrouped frequently to satisfy the instructional needs of each, a team organization is utilized. A team is a group of two or more teachers who assume the common responsibility for the total instructional program for two or more classrooms of children. Each team has the freedom to organize and group its students in the manner the teachers deem best. These teachers, complementing each other's talents, have common responsibility of planning, fulfilling and evaluating the total instructional program within the team. Back-to-back scheduling of the special teachers gives a team of teachers planning time during the week. Each team has four planning periods, 45 minutes in length, while their classes are taught by the specialists.

The children are placed in instructional groups in the team. For language arts children are grouped according to reading levels and skills. In mathematics, they are similarly grouped and regrouped according to changing skills and needs. By grouping students in this manner, each child has a better opportunity to work at his own achievement level at his own rate, and the overall range of achievement within a room is narrowed.

In homerooms, heterogeneous grouping (different ages and different levels) is used for science, social studies, and other areas of the curriculum. Each teacher attempts to help the children assigned to her to begin their work at their different levels and make as much progress as she can with each. At the end of the school year, not all of the children will have done the same work or completed the same books. After summer vacation each child begins where he left off in the spring.

Continuous progress requires that evaluation of growth be continuous. Careful observation and shifting from group to group and class to class makes it possible for each student to be placed where he can develop best.

How does the term "level" differ from the word "grade"? Grade denotes an expected achievement with a one-year time limit. Level denotes a group of skills and understandings learned without reference to a time limit.

In reporting to parents, teachers use telephone calls, conferences, progress reports and report cards. Since teachers prefer two-way communication, the telephone and conferences are used as much as possible.

The fulfillment of the goals of this nongraded program depends greatly upon the effective utilization of the special teachers. Through cooperative planning, the specialists can not only give instruction in their area of major interest but also enrich the overall program. Independent study and small group work helps children develop independence and responsibility. Activities of this type take place wherever space çan be found.

Each homeroom group is scheduled once a week for instruction in vocal music, physical education, and art. In addition to the regularly scheduled sessions with the homeroom groups, each specialist has some unscheduled time. During these periods the specialists work with large or small groups on special projects or give individual help as needed.

In addition to reading in a classroom situation, there is a corrective reading teacher who works with those who are having special reading problems.

Instrumental music classes are scheduled for a minimum of two times a week. One session is a small-group lesson on a particular instrument, while the other session is a large-group ensemble.

The teacher of sight-impaired children assists these children in furthering their intellectual and emotional growth. Special material and equipment is provided to help relieve eye strain. In meeting individual needs, speech and hearing therapy is also available to the students. Psychological services are used as a resource to the school to reinforce the instructional program by promoting optimum understanding of the child in order to further his adjustment and education, and the county health nurse visits the school frequently.

The pupil personnel worker is the liaison between the school and the home. His home visits help to meet the needs of individuals by interpreting the school program to parents for follow-up of specific problems or needs.

The Earth and Space Science Lab, which services the entire county, is housed in this building. In addition to scheduled visits to the planetarium, individuals at South Frederick can visit the lab to pursue special interests.

Teacher aides and volunteers play a very important role in the nongraded program. One of their duties is to assist teachers in audio-visual materials. Some of the aides type such things as experience stories dictated by the children. Aides also provide one-to-one relationships—one adult to one child. On-the-spot checking of student work is one of the duties of the aides. The work is given back to the child while the work is still fresh in his mind. Free play is supervised, and an aide in the classroom gives opportunity for two groups to have adult leadership. Some aides also do office work and prepare classroom work for teachers.

Volunteers assist with typing in the office and at home. They supervise children in the bus room and in the loading of buses.

As this nongraded plan was initiated, the walls of communication also came tumbling down. They had large attendance at all orientation sessions for parents. The frequently scheduled coffee hours provided informal opportunities to discuss the nongraded philosophy as it had been applied at the school.

The slide presentation concludes by stating that the organizational patterns of nongrading and team teaching, which promote the philosophy of continuous progress for each individual at his own rate, can be evaluated in terms of the development of skills and concepts, but the real evaluation of the nongraded program lies within the development of the inner self.

A Nongraded Middle School

In Columbia, Maryland, the Wilde Lake Middle School is housed in a climatically and acoustically controlled, open-space building enclosing 65,000 square feet of space, which includes three academic areas, a unified arts area, an instructional materials center, a performing arts area and planetarium, physical education facilities, a kitchen, a large commons area, and an administrative suite.

The school philosophy states that:

The faculty of Wilde Lake Middle School is building its educational program upon certain basic beliefs. These beliefs are derived from our experience and study in three contributing categories: the needs of society, the needs of the individual, and established learning theories.

We believe that each individual is unique and has varied capacities which the school should help him to develop to the fullest extent possible.

We believe in continuing progress for each student.

We believe the curriculum should be built to fit the student. The curriculum should be kept adaptable and flexible at all times, responsive to on-going evaluations.

We believe in the psychology of positive thinking. Ours is to be a success school for each student. Each staff member plays a significant role in the total guidance program of the school.

We believe in the dignity of the individual and in the mutual respect of human rights.

We believe our methods and materials should utilize a variety of resources and many learning modes to accommodate the individual needs of the students.

We believe the educational program should be the shared responsibility of the school, the home, and the student.[1]

This middle school is for students in the sixth, seventh, and eighth years of school, or ages twelve through fourteen. This is the educational home for over 700 students and a professional staff of 35. Each teacher has at least one competency area and a second interest to share with others.

The program applies the latest research findings concerning interdisciplinary team teaching, independent study, educational diagnosis and prescription, mastery of basic skills, contractual learning, and nongraded grouping. Teaching-learning strategies may be shared by both teacher and pupil. A reasonable attempt

---

[1] Used with permission from Charles L. Jones, Principal of Wilde Lake Middle School, Columbia, Maryland.

is made to find a program for each student. It is a place where a serious attempt is made to get students "tuned in" and "turned on" about learning.

Language arts, social studies and science teachers form an interdisciplinary team to develop units of study under the umbrella of a single concept. Because of the uniqueness of both language and skill, math is departmentalized. Four teachers of mathematics operate a continuous learning program in an area that supports the physical needs for multi-ability groupings. Related arts offers a diversified program to stimulate interest and permit talent development of students one-third of each day.

The students are ungraded throughout the school. They are grouped and regrouped both heterogeneously and homogeneously by ability depending upon the immediate task. All grouping is done by those who work directly with the students. Independent study can be an attraction for both talented and less talented students. Students with learning difficulties receive special assistance. A reading resource teacher works with small groups of students and is "on-call" for resource advice.

The school population is evenly divided into three PODS called Venus, Mars, and Jupiter. The nongraded PODS include students from each grade contained in the school. There is no power structure intended in any POD with appointments made by random selection. Team members work cooperatively to determine instructional needs, plans, strategies, and evaluations for each unit of study. There is always a unit under construction by a member of the teaching team; units are shared and exchanged from one team to another. A pre-test, post-test and student evaluation for each unit is commonplace.

A student applying for independent study privileges must satisfactorily answer the following: What is your goal? What materials will you need? What plan will you follow for checking-in with the teacher? What culminating activity do you propose which will permit others to share your findings?

The educational atmosphere is one of freedom which permits students and teachers to be responsible to one another for finding a balance between the cognitive and affective domains. Units of study focus on themes relevant to the needs and interests of students: human relations, conflict, power, revolution, ecology, decision making and risk taking, etc.

At the hub of the school is the Media Center, which is a place of action as well as an area for study removed from traffic. The use of the multi-media typifies this center.

Individual conferences are encouraged with the guidance role shared by many. The environment attempts to provide students with ample opportunities to ventilate feelings, voice opinions and work toward healthy interpersonal relations.

The student is afforded the opportunity to explore many of the various art media. The shop is organized to encourage the student to look beyond a tool or a project and fit such inquiry into a meaningful whole. Home economics is conducted in the kitchen and sewing rooms. Vocal music stimulates the here and now aspect of music enjoyment. Piano, guitar or rhythm instruments accompany the voice, and instrumental music is also enjoyed for both study and performance. Large instruments are furnished by the school, small horns belong to the students, and instruction is free.

Physical education supports both team and individual interests. The community facilities for tennis and swimming are shared by the students and afford another teaching station. The gymnasium is an arena for free play at noontime and is used almost every night by the Columbia Association, which plans a variety of recreational activities for residents.

Students are evaluated according to their individual growth as measured against their learning mode, talent, and habitual industry level. No grades are given. Students and teachers evaluate performance based upon behaviorally stated criteria, and significance is attached to any dialogue that takes place.

Club programs are absent at Wilde Lake Middle. Instead, special interests and talents are pursued in special interest groupings, which meet as part of the regular school day. After-school socials and intermurals replace nighttime dances and inter-scholastic sports.

Principal Charles Jones summarizes the operation of his school:

> We intend to humanize the learning act by daily dedicating ourselves to belief in the worth of the individual. If we are successful the student will begin to accept the responsibility for his own learning. The humanizing process naturally involves the student in decision-making. We hope that a practice of shared responsibilities will produce results which will have significant relevance for every student. We believe that learning should be exciting, continuous, unfragmented, and relative to the here and now. We believe that we tend to forget those things which we hear, we tend to remember those things which we see, and we tend to understand those things which we do. Wilde Lake Middle School is a doing school.

A Nongraded High School

As an open space school, Wilde Lake High School in Columbia, Maryland, is the first of its kind in secondary education. The philosophy of the school follows:

> The rate of change in today's society makes for a rate of adjustment hitherto unknown in the history and prehistory of MAN. Whether or not collective action can be taken to reduce the stress placed upon individuals remains surmise [sic]. If environments teach in the real

sense, and if each of us is a product of OUR infinite adjustments to our surroundings, then perhaps the new City of Columbia can produce a breed of individuals capable of living life more fully, more humanely. Wilde Lake High School is an outgrowth of such an environment.

Two factors, however, preclude the simplistic deduction that a school which grows out of an attempt to plan an intelligent environment for people will *ipso facto* produce a quality of graduate significantly better than its more traditional counterparts. (1) Students coming to the Wilde Lake High School spent their early years in environments quite different from the concept of Columbia, and the phenomenon of imprinting is a psychological and biological reality. (2) Columbia cannot be considered an "island" unto itself. It is part of a larger whole, and, as such, assumes the assets and liabilities of the total culture. The miracle of electronics makes us all a "victim" of small town interdependence. We cannot expect our students to escape fully the "pollution" of twentieth-century living.

The major responsibility of any school seems expressly the development of thinking and sensitive human beings capable of dealing intelligently with the vagaries of a complex technological environment. It is probable that no one human being can be expected to adjust to the exponential demand placed upon him by today's living without developing some form of DIS-ease. Ostensibly, we can help young people to understand what it means to be human and to remain so. They can then be encouraged to design their own environments conducive to their further development and maturity. The important accent should be placed upon activities and experiences which aid students to develop the competencies by which they can "take charge" of their own lives.

Wilde Lake High School will provide opportunities for each individual to develop according to his unique abilities and capacities and to appreciate his role in the development of his own species. Each person, however weakly, strives toward becoming a better functioning, more mature individual. A school program, if it is to be accountable to these differences, must be variegated, flexible, and able to adjust to whatever skills and learnings the students bring to school. Students will be afforded the opportunity to become more independent, to face choices, to make decisons as they learn to become more responsible for their own education.

Responsibility, like the more cognitive learnings, resides in students in differing quantities. The school will acknowledge these differences and attempt to provide individual students with a variety of experiences in their individual quests toward maturity. The respect each student associates with the successful completion of his commitments assumes a vital force in character development. The awareness that he has created something unique within his own craftsmanship is resident in the outward manifestations of his accomplishments. Making such commitments and keeping them will be given high priority throughout the facet of the school's program.

Involvement has become almost a cliché in the idiom of the day. Yet, involvement in the learning act by students seems an essential ingredient if education is to remain meaningful in their lives. The goal orientation of a previous era no longer seems applicable in an affluent society. Today's young people aren't likely to be engaged by subject matter and/or experiences which they do not perceive as relevant to their lives either present or future. Serious consideration as to how to make education socially and personally relevant will·be given.

The school will allow each student to choose the facilities and opportunities offered by the school that will be most beneficial to him. Each student needs opportunities to make decisions concerning what he will study, for what purpose, when he will study, what materials he will use, where he will study, and how he will judge the outcomes. Such an undertaking implies close relationships between the students and teachers. The idea of a secondary school teacher as strictly subject-matter oriented will be replaced by the notion of the teacher-advisor. Like their university counterparts, the teachers at Wilde Lake High School will assume responsibility for aiding students in planning their educational experiences so that they may gain the most from the opportunities resident in the school environment. Each teacher will be expected to accept, as collateral duty, the advisement of a given number of students—preferably multiage in grouping.

An atmosphere conducive to learning, on the part of the faculty and students alike, is created when individuals feel that they can try things out without fear of reprisal when the outcomes are not successful. A healthy respect for experimentation must prevail. Ideas will be encouraged and subject to continuing evaluation in light of their relationship to intended outcomes. Decision making, based upon good data, should permeate the activities of all individuals within the school.

A school which gives priority to the individual and his personal growth in a variety of ways must also take responsibility for helping him to gain a responsiveness to the feelings, the needs, the goals, and the hopes of others. Responsibility for others shall not be considered a glib generalization, but rather a value to be prized by the reward systems inherent in the school community.

Moreover, a student's responsibility for himself is not just limited to the decisions which influence his education. He needs to feel responsible for his actions within a group, and the actions of any group of which he is a part. The school should help him to develop responsibility to groups by allowing him to take part in decisions and subsequent actions by groups of his peers. The school should provide groups with guidance in understanding the role of the individual in group action. Such guidance should explicate the necessity for leadership and followership in group action. In sharing ideas and experiences, students learn to appreciate themselves and also develop an awareness of the value of others. Such group experiences provide enrichment for the individual in contributing to the enrichment of others.

Above all, the thread which runs through the entire school will emphasize the importance of communications. Probably no one aspect of human living is more important today for the successes of the individual and his collective species. Effective, efficient, and economic communications do not merely happen of themselves; they are nurtured in an environment which resounds their importance in its very existence. Being in touch with oneself and with others seems paramount in a world gone "mad" with change. If indeed the medium is the message, then the models that the school establishes for students in its everyday "clothing" speak more loudly than a hundred lines of rhetoric.

ASSUMPTIONS

1. Education is a process of facilitating a student's development toward independence. As students become more mature intellectually, they become less dependent on school personnel for direction.

2. As a developmental process, learning proceeds from many contexts, but inevitably must begin where a student is. As facilitators of learning, teachers should assist students to assess their entering behaviors and to help them construct learning environments appropriate to these assessments.

3. Every student has a natural curiosity for understanding his environment. A student already knows how to learn when he comes to school. The school's responsibility is to build on these competencies and to provide opportunities for students to encounter the world in depth and breadth.

4. Students learn more effectively when they see the relationship between what they are doing at the moment and where they might likely be at the end of a learning encounter.

5. In an affluent society, identity needs are more acute than survival needs. School experiences should be designed to help students discover more about themselves. It is through experiences that we come to understand ourselves.

6. When a student understands a 'subject' he is able to apply his learnings to a wider range of situations, and with a greater degree of flexibility. Therefore, he is not restricted to the immediate situation.[2]

NONGRADEDNESS:
AN EMERGING CONCEPT AT THE COLLEGE LEVEL

Many changes must be made in our educational programs to prepare teachers for today and tomorrow. To meet this challenge, prospective teachers must be aware of the full implications of the interrelationship of technology and social change, and of the impact of change upon educational patterns.

---

[2] Used with permission from Dr. John M. Jenkins, Principal of Wilde Lake High School, Columbia, Maryland.

Teachers must be willing to experiment, to seek more effective methods of education. Nongradedness is one such change in the educational pattern, and future teachers need to be prepared for this emerging philosophy.

Teachers are attempting to teach in a variety of organizational patterns. The best-planned organizatons do not function properly unless the teachers within them are prepared to make the transition from the graded, self-contained classroom to newer plans such as the nongraded, team-teaching organization.

Increased interest in nongradednesss has necessitated the need for greater understanding of how the nongraded school is being used and of the characteristics of teachers in nongraded schools. The needs of public schools could be better met if institutions preparing teachers had an awareness of the existing curricular structures and the nongraded techniques now being used.

If our new organizations are to make any real difference in the quality of education, then we must find ways to help teachers reconsider, adapt, or restructure their values about their roles in the learning process. I recently conducted a study and compiled the thinking of many teacher educators about the philosophy of nongradedness. The findings of this study illustrate the diversity of ideas held by many teacher educators in relation to nongradedness.

- Of those 773 institutions responding to the questionnaire, 21 institutions (2.7 percent) reported that they currently offer a specific course in "nongrading." Summer workshops in "nongrading" are offered by 13 institutions.

- In response to the question, "Does your institution currently consider 'nongrading' as a part of the content of one or more other courses?," 650 institutions (89.3 percent of those responding) replied in the affirmative and listed 1,468 such courses.

- Of the respondents, 76, or 9.8 percent, indicated that a course in "nongrading" is under consideration at their institutions. A new graduate program entitled, "The Child and the Individualized Curriculum," was described by one institution. Another described a nongraded community school program which is operated as part of the teacher-education program.

- Nongraded laboratory schools are operated by ten of the responding institutions and 45 institutions reported that they place student teachers in nongraded schools.

- The courses, workshops, and programs described indicate a concern of teacher educators about the importance of the nongraded philosophy. More than 90 percent of those participating in the study devote some time to teaching about nongradedness.

The common thread which was woven throughout the information and data collected from the questionnaires, correspondence and interviews, was the fact that teacher-educators are more and more viewing nongradedness as an emerging philosophy of education. Many institutions are applying the nongraded philosophy in organizing and conducting programs of teacher preparation. I shall briefly describe several of them.

The Education Division of Doane College, Nebraska, is beginning a continuous progress program of teacher education with no course titles.[3] Their program is competency based. Instructional units are divided into specific learning tasks, which each trainee completes at his own rate. Each unit includes statement of purpose, instructions, behavioral objectives, methods of evaluation, bibliography, and specific learning tasks.

---

[3] Richard E. Dudley, Chairman, Education Division, Doane College, Nebraska, private interview held during meeting of American Association of Colleges for Teacher Education, Chicago, Illinois, February 26, 1971.

Times for "education" are established within the student's schedule to permit arrangement of any seminars or other common experiences deemed feasible by the professors or the students. This also gives students specific times when they may utilize the resources within the "Education Labs" or in the Media Center when they will not have to compete with other students for the materials or equipment. This plan provides times within the student's schedule for assignment to public school classrooms for experience as a teaching assistant.

Students are scheduled regularly for small-group discussions and small-group work to improve student-professor relationships as well as student-student relationships. Human relations is a major concern of the staff at Doane. Individual conferences are scheduled biweekly to provide each trainee with guidance in planning and evaluating his own activities.

The Florida State University[4] design relies heavily on simulated experiences for trainees, including micro-teaching and opportunity for self-criticism. These activities are replacing the "methods courses." The philosophy is that students need practice in teaching.

Instead of teaching methods courses, the faculty is designing experiences for the trainees and gathering materials for use in such activities as micro-teaching, simulation, and video-taping. By planning excercises for the trainees to carry out rather than lessons and lectures, the professors are demonstrating commitment to teacher behavior, which emphasizes student rather than teacher involvement in learning activities. The program offers a variety of teaching strategies and styles. The student picks and chooses from these alternatives and tries them until he finds the one that best suits him.

This five-year program begins pre-service training in the

---

[4]Evelyn J. Blewett, *Elementary Teacher Training Models* (Washington, D.C.: U.S. Government Printing Office, 1969) pp. 22-30.

junior year. In-service training extends for three or four years of teaching after graduation. The cooperating public school teachers are appointed jointly by the University and the school system and are prepared for working with teacher trainees for two full-time summer sessions. They study new research on teaching effectiveness, new technology, and curriculum advancements in various academic fields of knowledge. By utilizing a computer, the University stores pertinent information on each trainee. The goals of the program are to help the prospective teacher to emerge as a skilled curriculum builder and to be able to assemble and organize a variety of teaching skills to meet the unique needs of the individuals he will teach.

The main concern of the teacher-education program at Michigan State University[5] is the importance of the future teacher having early experience with children. During the first and second years of the program the trainee works with children as an assistant teacher at the elementary school or in other settings such as scouting, children's hospital, or summer camp.

A prospective teacher has an experience as a member of a school "team," which consists of four experienced teachers, two student teachers, and one intern consultant or team leader. This team provides the instructional program for four elementary classrooms. The program is built upon the principles and techniques of the behavioral sciences and utilizes an inter-disciplinary approach. Content and instructional methods are presented as short, single-purpose experience modules. Each module is directed toward the accomplishment of a particular behavioral objective. These modules are grouped into clusters or "components." Over 2700 modules are included in the program. Modules are stored in a computer-processed information

---

[5] Ibid., pp. 36-39.

retrieval system and are utilized as needed by the trainees. Since these modules can be combined in numerous ways, programs are individualized according to individual learning styles or needs. Evaluation of each modular experience is tested for its contribution to a teacher's development and test results are compared with those of alternative experiences.

This is an undergraduate program with a one-year internship. The curriculum is divided into five interrelated general areas. The ultimate goal of the program is to develop creative teachers by promoting an attitude toward learning which fosters originality in working with children.

The planners of the University of Massachusetts[6] model for teacher training feel strongly that the student teacher needs practice in professional decision-making. They feel that teachers must be prepared for change. Features of this model include specific performance criteria, based on content knowledge, behavioral skills, and human relations skills. The program contains a strong emphasis on the human relations aspect of teaching.

Based on the assumption that each trainee's strengths and weaknesses differ and that they will also change during the program, continuous diagnosis of the needs of each is provided as well as continuous evaluation of the program components designed to meet these needs. There are multiple program alternatives to each objective. This diagnosis and evaluation is also made available to the graduate.

The ultimate goal of this program is to produce a fully human teacher who meets the human criteria of warmth and human understanding. This teacher should also be capable of rigorous thinking, be in control of his own behavior, and be in a

[6]Walt Le Baron, *Analytic Summaries of Specification for Model Teacher Education Programs* (Washington D.C.: U.S. Department of Health, Education and Welfare, 1969) pp. 71-87.

continuing pattern of growth. The teacher must also be a human-relations expert in addition to having content knowledge and a variety of teaching techniques.

Several major themes are indicated throughout the programs described. The major thrust is in practicing the philosophy of nongradedness. That is, if teachers are going to teach children in schools utilizing team teaching, continuous progress, non-grading, individualized instruction and modern technology, the teachers themselves should be trained in this manner. These programs are not only teaching about nongradedness, they are, in fact, nongraded programs of teacher education.

A major change seen in these programs is the performance orientation of the program. While traditional programs put great emphasis on entrance requirements, these competency based programs emphasize exit requirements. The logical explanation suggests that it is more relevant to examine a prospective teacher's abilities after completion of a program than before he enters it. Teachers are recommended for certification on the basis of performance, rather than on the basis of completion of specified courses.

The individualized approach described in these programs emphasizes the importance of the teacher-trainee's planning, directing, and evaluating his own program. Through inquiry and discovery, each develops his own style of teaching. Opportunities are provided for each prospective teacher to assume individual responsibility for his own study and learning.

Teacher-education is viewed as a process of continuous training throughout a teacher's career. Plans are made to include local school districts so that in-service can become an integral part of this continuous training. There is a trend toward early and continuous field experiences so that the prospective teacher begins to work with children at the initial stages of the program

A closer cooperation appears to exist between the training institutions and the public schools. While the schools are used for settings of practical experiences for the student-teacher, the regular teachers are utilizing the resources of the university to upgrade their teaching techniques and methods.

The sharing of responsibilities for decision-making for programs of teacher-education represents a growing trend. There appears to be greater cooperation between all concerned: the college, the students, the public schools, the community, educational governmental agencies, state departments of education, foundations, teachers' associations, etc.

Human relations is also a major concern. Recognizing that the prospective teacher must learn how to work with groups of people—students and colleagues, both children and adult—the trainees are provided with experiences in interpersonal relations, sensitivity training, and the group process. The ultimate goal is that the trainee will not only become skilled in methods and techniques, but also in human relations.

The development of personalized teacher-education programs such as those described here demonstrates that individualized programs can be instituted so that different sequences of preparation can be prescribed for different prospective teachers. These developments represent the contributions of teams of scholars working to completely revise teacher education, by designing new models to meet the unique needs of individuals. This indicates a sincere commitment to the emerging philosophy of nongradedness.

—SUMMARY—

The nongraded school represents an endeavor to facilitate through organization a plan for the continuous growth of people. The nongraded organization is a vertical one which provides for differentiated rates and means of progression toward achievement of educational goals.

The primary function of a nongraded program should be to provide an environment that will enhance the development of values and attitudes. There should be many opportunities for a growing, responsible independence, with each student gradually accepting more responsibility for his own learning and assuming greater self-direction. Emphasis should be placed on the personal development of the individual and on self-understanding.

The nongraded curriculum becomes an organized series of experiences based upon the needs of the learner to provide for his continuous growth and development toward desirable goals and objectives. The purpose of these learning activities is to enable each student to acquire and develop skills, abilities, understandings, and attitudes that will help him to live effectively and happily in his environment.

Included here are recommendations for changing to a nongraded program and brief descriptions of a nongraded elementary school, a nongraded middle, a nongraded high school, and nongrading at the college level.

The basic tenet of the philosophy of the open classroom is that education is a live-in. Each person is uniquely different. Meeting individual differences is not a technique; it is a way of living. It includes accepting others, respecting their contributions, working for the kind of group operation in which each individual knows he has a part, and encouraging each to give his best in each situation. Because nongradedness is concerned with meeting individual needs, it has become a vehicle for creating open classrooms.

chapter seven | Team Teaching and the Open Classroom

The philosophy of the open classroom includes the idea that most human learning is the result of interrelationships of human beings as they develop in social situations. Team teaching enhances the development of this idea.

DEFINITION OF TEAM TEACHING

There are many definitions and descriptions of team teaching. Quite a few have been printed in various educational magazines and textbooks. To many, team teaching means only the using of large- and/or small-group instruction. Others see it as a hierarchy of personnel having a designated team leader with other teachers as subordinates, each with a different function in the area of his special competence. To some it means two teachers working together with equal responsibility.

Simply stated, a team is a group of two or more teachers who assume the common responsibility for the total instructional program for a group of students. These teachers plan together, teach together, and evaluate together.

The children as well as the teachers make up the team and there is a close working relationship among teachers of a team. Teachers group and regroup pupils frequently to satisfy the instructional needs of each individual. A team organization provides for more productive planning and sharing of the instructional process and thus leads to more efficient and interesting ways of presenting educational experiences.

Since the teachers are concerned more with concepts and generalizations than they are with facts, the team approach helps students "uncover" the subject matter, rather than have the teachers "cover" it.

ADVANTAGES OF TEAM TEACHING

The advantages claimed for team teaching are many. Some of the advocates of team teaching tell us that research and experience have shown that grade-level grouping in self-contained classrooms for all learning is both ineffective and inefficient. They state that some lessons can be taught better in a large group, and a group of teachers, working together to share the responsibility of a large group of children, can better meet the needs of all children. In many schools the children and teachers have been divided into teams spanning more than one grade level, and the schedules are arranged so as to permit children to work in another team when it seems advantageous to do so. Also a point on the positive side of team teaching is the fact that elementary school teachers, who had been finding it impossible to keep abreast of new knowledge in all areas of the curriculum, are now able to do this with teammates sharing the total responsibility. Each teacher on a team assumes the major responsibility for one or two areas of the curriculum and keeps the others "up-to-date."

Team teaching encourages flexibility due to the possibility of providing more variety in assignments, scheduling, grouping and space. This organizational plan facilitates specialization in teaching. Each may plan and teach in his area of special interest and expertise.

Team teaching also provides for improvements in supervision. Teachers have reported that they find teaming stimulating because they have the opportunity to watch other teachers at work. This arrangement also gives the individual teacher some time to herself while other team members are teaching in a large-group situation. Still others contend that the organizational scheme allows the teacher more time to give individual help to students who need it. The plan includes ways of utilizing teacher aides, volunteers and other resource personnel. Team teaching has been found helpful in working with disadvantaged children because teachers have more time to give attention to students with specific problems.

Some children have been motivated just by the change of rooms and teachers. Children have the advantage of the skilled teacher for part of the day instead of being with the inexperienced one all day long. It is also reported that pupils are able to spend more time working with a teacher because when they are divided into smaller groups, there is more opportunity for the teacher to work with each group.

Teachers in schools with team-teaching programs report that they feel they know their pupils better and, therefore, can give more individual attention to them. They feel that team teaching provides more individualization of instruction.

AN EXAMPLE OF A TEAM-TEACHING PLAN

In a typical team-teaching school, one might see the following organization:

The pupils are grouped heterogeneously for social studies and science. Variances in the capabilities of children are taken care of by the wide range of texts and other materials provided for them, instructional tasks at various levels of difficulty, and opportunities to explore their own interests.

For the "skill" subjects—language arts and mathematics—the pupils are grouped and regrouped on the basis of past achievement and on suggested levels by previous teachers. They are regrouped as their needs change. This regrouping means close coordination and continuous planning by teachers.

The team plans for comprehensiveness, sequence, improved methods, meeting individual needs, preparation of creative materials, and opportunities for large- and small-group instruction. There is no predetermined arrangement for teachers to combine classes for large-group instruction; rather, such occasions are dictated by the development of the curriculum as appropriate learning opportunities are planned.

For skill subjects teachers usually work in separate classrooms or in separate parts of an open-space area with their particular groups for the lesson. Occasionally, one teacher will take part of another teacher's group for an activity while the other teacher helps a smaller group with a special project. Often, teachers plan to co-teach every day. In this case, the two teachers organize all the pupils at several learning stations, such as a listening station or skill table, and then move from group to group.

Within the framework of the various groupings, continuous evaluation of pupils takes place. No one group is static. During the course of the year, pupil groupings will vary greatly. At times, pupils will be members of fast-moving, high-achievement groups in certain phases of the program. At other times, they will be members of groups designed to meet specific developmental needs in the skills. The interaction of teachers with pupils and teachers with teachers is a vital aspect of evaluation in a continuous progress plan.

DIFFERENTIATED STAFFING

Team teaching is an organizational pattern that promotes flexibility and encourages the individualization of instruction. The team approach implies the utilization of special teachers, teacher aides, volunteers, and peer teachers. It becomes a cooperative venture.

Fulfillment of the goals of open education depends greatly upon the effective utilization of special teachers. Through cooperative planning, specialists can not only give instruction in their area of major interest but also enrich the overall program.

Each child is naturally creative. Through creating he expresses himself and finds release from inner tensions. The special subjects provide much opportunity for developing this creativity. In addition to individual attention to specific needs, these areas involve group activities in which the individual, by himself, cannot complete the task at hand. Although each player plays and each singer sings, it is not a band or chorus until it is the group acting as one. A mural is painted by many and each must work individually, but all must work in harmony toward a common goal under a common leadership.

Art is a vital part of the open classroom. An art program should be designed to fit each student's needs and provide for independent thinking. Art is for everyone, not just a select few, and each child should have the opportunity to develop to the extent of his interests and abilities. From our knowledge of individual differences has come the conviction that each child's art should reflect his uniqueness. Children learn about art in relation to their needs and interests. The learning rate, the material mastered and the nature of the work vary greatly within any group of children. We must provide variation in every art experience as children experiment with new materials.

Each child is creative, but each in different degrees and different ways. This creativity needs to be encouraged and developed. We must provide creative opportunity for each child so that he can become more independent and resourceful in his thinking as he uses a variety of art materials to express himself. Art activities in the open classroom should be on a personal and individual basis, with emphasis on flexibility. The art center should be a "beehive" of activity at all times.

Music is a creative, expressive impulse that is born in every normal child. That is what music education is for: to help children use their musical powers to create not only more life but also a better life. There is something in music for every individual. Music is *in* people, it comes *from* people, and it is *about* people, it is *for* people. Individuals vary in their ability to learn rhythmic coordination and vocal achievement. These needs should be met through culminating activities, such as programs utilizing the best talents and cooperation of each child. While some children sing, others should dramatize and play instruments.

The total music program should provide experience in singing, rhythms, playing instruments, creative activities, guided listening, harmonic experiences, and advanced guidance and cooperation in band and chorus. This will enable each child to find some area of musical expression which will continue into adult life. In addition to regularly scheduled visits, individuals and small groups should be able to visit the music center to pursue special interests.

Instrumental music is a part of the total curriculum. Classes should be scheduled for those students who wish to take advantage of the opportunity to perform on any string, wind, or percussion instrument. The instrumental teacher should meet frequently with parents and take an active part in community affairs so that music can make a contribution to the social, mental, and spiritual development of the child.

Physical education experiences should also be included in the program because these experiences are important to the child's complete development and because they can do things for a child that other areas of the curriculum cannot do. All of a child's responses, whether they be intellectual, emotional, social, or physical, are interrelated.

Although the major function of physical education is to help children keep well and grow strong through participation in physical activities, it also has other purposes that are related to social and personal development. The program has as its purpose the development of the whole personality of each child—physical, social, and emotional. The areas of social development that are especially benefited concern desirable attitudes and an understanding of the role of a member of a group. Physical education prepares boys and girls to participate in wholesome physical recreation and helps them develop concepts and habits of healthful living. In addition to regularly scheduled periods, individuals and small groups should be able to visit the physical education center at other times to pursue special interests.

The basic responsibility of a public school is to attempt to educate each child to the full extent of his capacity. In order to carry out this philosophy, it is sometimes necessary to provide special services and programs when a child has a problem that cannot be handled within the regular classroom situation. For a number of reasons, there are pupils within the school who are not reading in keeping with their capacity level. Many of these cases can be identified and corrected in the regular classroom program. In many cases, specialized help is needed outside the regular program to supplement the developmental reading program.

The reading specialist should work with all of the teachers to help identify specific needs, to suggest special materials and methods, and to teach individuals and small groups. The role of this specialist is that of a resource person for the entire school. The goal—that each pupil may function at his highest capacity in the total school curriculum—will be realized through the cooperative efforts of every teacher involved in the educational program of all children.

Classroom teachers are trained to teach individuals, yet when there are individuals in a class with physical or mental differences that cause the child to be unable to satisfactorily participate within the group, we cannot expect the classroom teacher to be a speech therapist, a teacher of the deaf, blind, partially sighted, orthopedically handicapped, mentally retarded, or emotionally disturbed. When an individual participating in a group has a physical or mental problem severe enough to need special isntruction, the services of special teachers are called upon.

The teacher of partially sighted children assists these children in furthering their physical development and in guiding their intellectual and emotional growth. The specialist teaches health education by helping the child become aware of the components of an adequate diet, the value of adequate rest and good posture, and the knowledge of safety factors related to limited vision. The student is aided in further developing other senses used as substitutes for sight when possible, and in the maximum use of residual vision without undue eyestrain. Proficiency is developed in listening, following directions, self-activity, travel and mobility, and group participation, as well as in academic areas. The teacher of vision-impaired children teaches each child to admit that he has a handicap and shows him how to adjust to it. The child is taught to plan constructively on the basis of his limitation, make wise choices, and deal with his anxieties and tensions by taking positive steps toward relieving them. He is helped to understand that it is a lifetime adjustment and that time and practice can make the adjustment easier.

Speech and hearing therapy is one of a number of pupil services now available to students in public schools. All teachers are aware that a child who has overcome speech and hearing handicaps is a more receptive child to teach. Often, improvement in speech results in higher achievement, a finer attitude toward school, fewer emotional, social and mental problems in daily life, and increased confidence in abilities.

Speech therapy is a highly specialized program of identification and remediation for individuals whose speech deviates consistently and conspicuously from normal speech to the extent that it calls attention to itself, interferes with communication, or causes maladjustment. Therapy is a process involving a change in behavior to achieve the best oral communication possible for the individual. It is based on an eclectic approach to theories and methods and the utilization of those theories and methods most appropriate in each case. Basic to therapy is the ability to view an individual as a person in his environment and to be concerned with each factor that relates to the cause and maintenance of the speech problem. The focus must be on the individual situation rather than on the deviation.

Within an educational setting it would seem logical that two of the principal pathways to learning—hearing and speech—would be important. Any disruption of these two processes interferes with learning. This concern has stimulated a progressive movement for providing speech and hearing services in public schools. These services provide for identification, assessment, and treatment for individuals handicapped by disorders of communication. Speech and hearing therapists have been employed by local boards of education to assume these responsibilities.

In order to function effectively, the therapist must have an understanding of the total school philosophy and the goals and principles related to the learning process. In other words, the therapist must cultivate a sense of readiness, motivation, performance, and application. His specific skills and professional identity must remain that of the specialist offering services to children with significant speech and hearing disorders.

Psychological services are offered primarily as a resource to the school to reinforce the instructional program by promoting optimum understanding of the child in order to further his adjustment. The services should include:

1. Evaluation of children being considered for special education for the following reasons: physical handicap, mental retardation, severe mental defect.
2. Evaluation of pupils who are referred through the school because of poor adjustment.
3. Consultation with the pupil-personnel worker whose concern is with problems originating in liaison service between home and school.

The program of the pupil-personnel worker is organized on the premise that all children should attend school regularly and thereby profit from the benefits of education. The uniqueness of each individual child is prominent in the thinking of the pupil-personnel worker; thus, the philosophy of pupil personnel is based on the singularity and value of each child as a worthy individual who should have confidence in his own ability to acquire full self-realization. Since all behavior is caused and the causes can be multiple, the teacher is the key person in recognizing symptomatic behavior and in supporting the case-work of the pupil-personnel service.

The duties of the pupil-personnel worker necessitate close working relationships with the school staff. He is the liaison between the school and the home. His home visits help promote good public relations not only through interpretations of the school program but also because he is working individually with the child. The pupil-personnel worker is very much an integral part of the teaching team.

Special teachers are very important members of a teaching team. With some flexibility in the scheduling and some extra time allotted, the specialists work with individuals and large and small groups on special projects and programs in addition to their regular classroom instruction. The method by which they are scheduled gives them opportunities to help meet the needs of children when, together with other members of the staff, general and specific curricular needs have been determined.

The success of open classrooms depends greatly on activities and experiences provided by specialists working closely with the total staff on the total school program, which is geared to meeting individual needs in open classrooms.

—SUMMARY—

A team is a group of two or more teachers who assume the common responsibility for the total instructional program for a group of students. These teachers plan together, teach together, and evaluate together.

A team organization provides for more productive planning and sharing of the instructional process, and thus leads to more efficient and more interesting ways of presenting experiences.

Team teaching is an organizational pattern that promotes flexibility and encourages individualization of instruction. The team approach implies the utilization of special teachers, teacher aides, volunteers, and peer teachers. It becomes a cooperative venture.

Fulfillment of the goals of open education depends greatly upon the effective utilization of special teachers. Through cooperative planning, specialists can not only give instruction in their area of major interest but also enrich the overall program. Team teaching enhances the development of open classrooms.

chapter eight || Learning Centers and the Open Classroom

The concept of learning centers is an organizational format for arranging instructional activities to provide greater opportunities for individualized teaching and to facilitate independent learning in open classrooms.

In his book, *Invitation to Learning: The Learning Center Handbook*, Ralph Voight says:

> The Learning Center, fully developed, implies certain characteristic behaviors on the part of the teacher, an enlarged learning environment, greater independence on the part of the learner, and revised physical arrangements in the classroom. The Learning Center of the future embodies the implementation of an idea—each child will grow at his own rate, in his own style, and to his uniquely personal potential. The Learning Center can provide a highly personal experience for the child, and can facilitate learning through a feedback system. The Learning Center within this pattern becomes a process offering an orderly, contextual experience.
>
> Through the Learning Center method of ordering a classroom, the teaching act may involve just one teacher or all the teachers on a

173

staff. A teacher, in concert with the principal and/or a curriculum specialist, may elect to establish Learning Centers. He may wish to add a few Centers in a regular self-contained classroom choosing to emphasize material for Centers that support a basic skill program or which relate to a unit of study in Social Studies or Science, or merely add a complementary or enriching element to the classroom.

On the other hand, the teacher may elect to alter his course and convert his self-contained, somewhat traditional classroom and methodology to a total Learning Center scheme in which case the types and numbers of Centers are increased proportionately.

Another organizational configuration might involve a grouping of two or more teachers. A team or cooperative teaching arrangement between or among teachers might adopt total or partial Learning Center instruction. Finally, an entire building might decide to convert to a Learning Center method of teaching.

Since Learning Centers aim at individuality, a Center in the "second grade" ought to be useful to any other child if it fits his maturity, interests, and learning style without regard to grade level. Learning Centers can be a stepping stone to "ungrading" or "non-grading" a school. This process may begin at grades K-3, or it may go school-wide—but Learning Centers can help.[1]

THE LEARNING-CENTER APPROACH

The goals and purposes of the open classroom could best be served by open-space learning centers, and the use of interdisciplinary teaching teams. By placing students and teachers in one area where they could work together easily, give suggestions to each other, hear each other and help each other, all would benefit.

Students would be involved in planning for meeting their own needs, and teachers would plan together to create the best possible learning atmosphere. All teachers would have their

[1] Ralph C. Voight, *Invitation to Learning: The Learning Center Handbook* (Washington, D.C.: Acropolis Books Ltd., 1971) pp. 2-5.

personal work areas located in a central room. This en inter-staff communication, not only in terms of a par child's situation, but in general "togetherness." The staff, ... not necessarily having to have congruent ideas in implementation, must feel good about and unthreatened by each other.

Each teacher would implement studies in her field and would not be expected to be a specialist in other fields. Thus, each teacher could concentrate study and preparation in the area for which she is responsible. This, per se, is not departmentalization in that all subjects are not viewed as such, but are rather a body of knowledge in process. Furthermore, each child's schedule will be unique to him. Classes should not be scheduled from center to center and period to period.

The learning center is essentially an actual geographical location where a child can work independently with a series of related activities, which are designed to promote independent understanding of certain concepts. The teachers assist students where necessary in the selection of appropriate centers and activities. Ultimately, the child will develop the ability to schedule himself and discipline himself to carry out his own scheduled activities. This includes self-directed movement throughout the building to appropriate learning areas according to schedules that have been formed by the child the previous day. His progress would be recorded in each learning center and codified among homeroom teachers. A period of time at the beginning of each day should be used for planning and a period of time at the end of each day should be used for evaluating.

There should be some type of homeroom organization to handle administrative matters and to provide for identification with a smaller peer group and with a teacher, even though pupils will be moving into various groupings throughout the day (large-group activity, small-group activity, individualized instruction, independent study, etc.).

Children will need a period of time—probably several months—to understand and utilize fully the freedom of moving from center to center and learning to form personal responsibility for large periods of time during the day. Some children are able to handle this type of freedom almost immediately, while others will always need some guidance. Teacher-pupil conferences should be fully utilized in guiding pupils to choose the best experiences for meeting their needs. A good deal of the scheduling for the centers will be done by instructional groups and planned with the teachers in the centers. Children need to be taught how to use their freedom. They cannot just be told to "do their thing."

Learning-Center Teams

Each learning center should house all the books, materials, equipment, and other resources (including the human resource of teachers, aides, and other personnel) which pertain to the particular discipline of the center.

In each learning center the teaching team should be charged with the responsibility of planning all the activities of its center. These plans include analyzing needs, prescribing activities, and evaluating progress. For example, the math team should arrange for instruction and guidance of all the children who come to the math center. The experiences and materials should be so varied that any child could come to the center with any math-related problem and find the necessary activity to help him solve his problem in such a way that the learning experience would be relevant to him.

In each center the teaching team should provide many self-directing activities. A child should be able to come to the center and proceed independently with pre-arranged instructions. One teacher could be working with a group on a particular skill which is a common need of those in the group; another teacher could be involved in a one-to-one conference with a child; another teacher could be engaged in professional reading or preparation of future "center" activities; an aide could be available to those children working on independent activities; a group of children could be viewing a film—the possibilities are limitless and could all be happening simultaneously. The center should be alive with activity. Instead of doing meaningless busy work, children should be seeking relevant solutions to real problems.

The Instructional Materials Center

The Instructional Materials Center, with all its available resources, human and material, should exist to further the objectives of the learning-center teams. All persons in the school team, adults and children, should find it easy and satisfying to use the center. The center should be directed, organized, staffed, and housed so that the needs of the school and the neighborhood that it serves will be met effectively.

Where the real purpose of the IMC is understood by everyone in the school, the center becomes an essential element in operating a good instructional program in every learning center, in extracurricular activities and in the homes of the community.

The school library is incorporated as an integral part of the IMC. The basic function of the center is not just the selection, management and circulation of books; rather, it is one of assistance in helping the teaching team to perform the instructional process most effectively through making all kinds of books, materials and equipment available.

The IMC is the heart of the instructional program, as most

school activities become associated with the library. A good center includes not only reading but many other activities as well. It is the main instructional aids center including audio-visual materials and equipment.

The services of the instructional materials center should:

- teach children to use basic library procedures and skills;
- suggest teaching aids appropriate for the instructional program;
- provide leadership in selecting, organizing, housing, and using library materials;
- help children in assigned and recreational reading;
- provide reading materials for individual children;
- prepare and distribute book lists, filmstrip guides, etc.;
- provide information concerning library materials available from other sources;
- make arrangements to borrow materials from other sources.

A good school must have an IMC that operates as a center of teaching services and instructional materials. It must be the heart of the instructional program. Everyone in the school (teachers, students, parents and the community) should find it easy and satisfying to use the services provided.

IMC personnel must be completely involved in cooperative working relationships with all other members of the instructional staff in planning how the center is to be used. The coordinator of the center should have at least one full-time assistant. The center staff must be well-acquainted with the nature and purposes of modern education and must share in all professional in-service activities. As accepted members of the teaching staff, they need to be involved in curriculum planning to be able to participate intelligently in classroom activities and to be able to conduct their service so that it is an integral part of the school environment for learning.

Materials implement, enrich and support our educational programs. A wide range of materials on all levels of difficulty, presenting many points of view and varied understandings and backgrounds, is necessary to meet the needs of individual students. The selection of appropriate instructional materials to be used by pupils is a major responsibility of the coordinator of the IMC.

The newer methods of teaching make greater demands on the IMC than have ever been made before. The trend toward using more and varied materials is unmistakable, and the various plans of supervised study and the long-range assignments demand increased reading materials. Provisions must be made to check out many books and materials for long periods of time. Some of the material could remain in the learning centers as a permanent collection; other materials should be transferred from the IMC for the period needed and replaced at the close of the study.

In addition to the plan of lending materials to the learning centers for the duration of a particular study or activity, other methods of making materials available are: having children leave the learning centers and come to the IMC individually during class time; having groups and classes come to the IMC during class time; placing books on reserve shelves. The most satisfactory methods appear to be those of developing libraries in each learning center and of sending pertinent materials as needed. This type of service demands a coordinator who keeps in touch with the work of the centers. He must be familiar with modern methods of teaching and should not be unduly concerned if a few books disappear when they are freely available in the learning centers and in the open stacks in the library.

An IMC cannot be wholly succesful unless the teachers are aware of its resources, see the possibilities of its use as an instructional aid, and encourage its use through the procedures they employ in their teaching. The use of the IMC by the teachers themselves is one of the best ways of encouraging children to use it.

The facility for the IMC should be as large as possible and preferably in the center of the building to provide easy access from all other areas. There needs to be adequate shelving for a large collection of library books, small seminar rooms, a "living room" corner to encourage recreational reading, places for individuals and small groups to use audio-visuals, filing space for pictures and other instructional materials, typing and duplicating facilities, work space for groups and individuals, display areas for creative work and racks for displaying paperbacks.

Because of the complexity of the IMC, the variety of materials housed there and the constant need for children and adults to visit, there should be no regularly scheduled time for class groups. Rather, anyone and everyone should be afforded the opportunity to visit the IMC whenever and as often and for as long as there is a need.

Individualized Schedules

Since each child's growth pattern is different from all others, his schedule should be unique to him and his needs. One child may complete an activity in 15 minutes while another child may require an hour to do the same task. Because of this diversity, I would suggest the use of a modular schedule; that is, divide the school day into blocks of time (15 or 20 minutes long). This would allow each child to schedule himself for the length of time that he feels would be necessary for him to complete an activity.

A child may wish to plan a project that will last several weeks. With this type of scheduling he can plan time each day to pursue this particular interest. For example, he may want to make a puppet out of papier mâché. This would require a short period of work time each day with an overnight drying time. Another child may wish to concentrate on a special project, and he could schedule himself for an afternoon or perhaps an entire day for his activity. For example, the editor of the school paper may need to spend a day setting up the "dummy" and making arrangements for the printing of the paper.

If a child is very interested in music, he may schedule himself for more activities in the music center than would another child who would prefer more art work. With modular scheduling each child can have more opportunities to pursue his major interests. Modular scheduling thus serves to promote self-direction and self-discipline because each pupil can plan his own time to meet his own needs, to satisfy his own curiosities, and to develop more depth in his areas of major interest.

During the planning and evaluation periods, the teachers should carefully guide each child so that he will not schedule himself too heavily in one area to the neglect of another. The teacher needs to have faith in the child. She should assume that he will utilize his time wisely and give him the freedom to plan his schedule. If and when you, the teacher, find that the pupil needs guidance, help him to formulate a well-rounded schedule. Don't do it for him. Don't tell him what to do and when; but help him to see the value of using time wisely.

A sample of a child's schedule is shown in Figure 8-1. The time blocks with the "X" mark on them indicate the parts of the schedule that were planned during a teacher-pupil conference, because of the on-going experiences of her instructional group, or because of the specific times allocated for certain activities (e.g., instrumental music must be scheduled when the band teacher is available, or student council meets every Friday at 12:30). The schedule for Monday is completely planned. The child then plans for the unscheduled modules day by day as needs dictate for the rest of the week.

NAME Susie Smart DATE Oct. 14-18

MODULE	MONDAY	TUESDAY	WEDNESDAY	THURSDAY	FRIDAY
8:30	Plan	Plan	Plan	Plan	Plan
8:45	Plan	Plan	Plan	Plan	Plan
9:00	S.S. Center (14)	Lang. Arts Center (5)	Art		
9:15	S.S. Center (14)	Lang. Arts Center (5)	Art		
9:30	I.M.C.		Art		
9:45	S S Center				
10:00	Seminar				
10:15	Seminar			SS Center	
10:30	Math Center (6)	Math Center (11)		Large Group Film	
10:45	Math Center (6)	Math Center (11)		Seminar	
11:00	Math Center (9)			Seminar	Music
11:15	Math Center (9)				Music
11:30	Math Center (9)	Lunch			Music
11:45	Lunch	Lunch	Evaluation	Lunch	I.M.C.
12:00	Lunch	P.E.		Lunch	Lunch
12:15	I.M.C.	P.E.			Lunch
12:30	I. M.C.		Activities		Student
12:45	Instrumental			Instrumental	Council
1:00	Instrumental		(Teacher	Instrumental	
1:15	Sci. Center (37)		Planning)		
1:30	P.E.				
1:45	P.E.				
2:00	P.E.				
2:15	Lang. Arts Center (2)				
2:30	Lang. Arts Center (2)			P.E.	P.E.
2:45	Lang Arts Center (2)			P.E.	P.E.
3:00	Evaluation	Evaluation		Evaluation	Evaluation
3:15	Evaluation	Evaluation		Evaluation	Evaluation

Figure 8-1

Learning Stations

Many educators claim that team-teaching programs that promote continuous progress of children can be conducted only in a modern building because of the flexibility required. True, the goals and purposes of team teaching in learning centers can best be served by an open-space building. However, a modern facility is not a prerequisite to such a program. The building is far less important than the human element involved. Traditional buildings can be renovated by taking out some walls and by adding acoustical treatment.

Learning centers can be established in traditional buildings even without renovation. Each center can be in a certain section of a building and can include several classrooms. Although it would not be as convenient and expedient in permitting children to move freely from center to center throughout the building, it is possible to utilize an old "egg crate" school in a more effective manner. The success of a program should be evaluated in terms of what is happening to children, rather than what kind of facility is being used.

Within each learning center are learning stations, which are activities that lead to the mastery of a skill or the understanding of a certain concept. These activities provide opportunities for a child to work independently. Ultimately, a child will develop the ability to schedule himself and discipline himself to carry out his own scheduled activities.

Learning stations provide opportunities for children of varying abilities and interests to experience success. By sharing different procedures, ideas and solutions to problems, children will develop alternative ways of reaching an objective. Learning stations provide sharing experiences.

One of the most important aspects of the learning station concept is that it provides the child with an environment in which he is free to make choices. This open classroom atmosphere encourages the child to choose from among alternatives—how he will solve a problem, which issues he wants to pursue in depth, when he wants to do certain stations, which materials he wants to use, where he will get the materials, how he will evaluate his activities, etc.

The "Quanswer" Idea

A teacher and a group of children developed this idea to provide more depth in many stations. The "quanswer" is a combination of questions and answers. The symbol used to designate quanswer is Ω

The quanswer consists of a continual questioning of the answer until the child has exhausted all possible ramifications of the question. For example, the following could appear in the activities of a station:

$$\Omega \text{ Felony}$$

The child looks up the definition of felony. He finds the answer: "Any of various offenses graver than a misdemeanor."

Ω What is an offense?

Answer: - - - - - - - - -

Ω What is a misdemeanor?

Answer: - - - - - - - - -

Ω What does grave mean?

etc. . . .

Eventually, all possibilities are exhausted and only the original question remains. Ultimately, the child will incorporate all the above information in the more sophisticated context of a paragraph. This assures that the learning station will not be simply verbalized; it will be an in-depth understanding of a problem or concept.

PLANNING STATIONS AND CENTERS

The first step in the planning for stations and centers is the development of guidelines, goals and objectives to be considered in establishing this organizational arrangement. Such guidelines should include the following:

- the most meaningful learning takes place through the process of discovering for oneself;
- individuals draw relationships from their backgrounds of experience;
- individuals react to a stimulus and initiate action at their own rate and depth;
- learning takes place best when the individual has freedom of choice;
- there is a direct relationship between meaningful learning and amount of personal involvement;
- learning situations need to be provided at many levels;
- each child must have opportunities to think and work as an individual as well as a member of a group;
- learning takes place best when an individual assumes responsibility for his own program of instruction.

The next step involves organizing for the use of stations. Once the decision has been made concerning organization—one teacher in a self-contained room, a team approach, stations for part of the day, stations completely, etc.—the next step is consideration of the physical arrangements.

It is not necessary to have all new furniture. One can use learning stations without any additional furniture. Stations can be put on bulletin boards, sides of file cabinets, easels, chalkboards, chart racks, or mounted on cardboard and suspended from the ceiling with heavy string. Student desks and tables can be arranged to become the bases for cardboard boxes on which stations are placed.

Figure 8-2

The next step is determining the activities by planning a variety of individual assignments at various levels of difficulty. The stations should provide opportunities for children to work with basic skills, facts, concepts, and large ideas. Some of the activities should be open-ended to provide for the development of problem-solving techniques, critical thinking and creativity. Some activities should lead to the construction of stations by students.

Some stations should be teacher-taught; others should be student-directed. Each station should include simplified, clear-cut statements of objectives, directions, activities, and methods of evaluation. Many manipulative items should be available. Some stations should be assigned; others should be student-selected.

The final stages of preparing for the use of learning stations include the development of plans for assignment, evaluation, record keeping, and teaching children how to use stations.

Sample Learning Stations

(Several close-up pictures of learning stations, with descriptions will be included on the next several pages.)

Figure 8-3

Figure 8-4

Figure 8-5

Figure 8-6

Figure 8-7

Figure 8-8

Figure 8-9

Figure 8-10

HOW TO INITIATE THE LEARNING-CENTER APPROACH

There is no one way to begin. Teachers should plan the approach that best suits them. Voight describes several minicase histories of successful classroom transitions to the learning-center organization:

Double room with no dividing wall. A first and second grade class began school in the fall with the Learning Centers already set up. The teacher, using a brief total class orientation period then introduced the Centers one by one to small groups of children.

Cooperative teaching experiences in separate rooms. Two fourth grade teachers worked with children to develop appropriate attitudes and work habits before using the Center method. The introduction of Centers began with a single Center and grew with new Centers being added from time to time until the entire program was carried on by the Learning Center Teaching Method.

Self-contained sixth grade. After much thought and a great deal of physical preparation, a teacher planned a week's orientation period with the children and then made a complete change to Centers at the beginning of the second week.

Team teaching in separate rooms. The teachers in the team designed the Centers and set them up at the beginning of the school year. The introduction to the Centers consisted of planning and discussion periods during the time normally spent on opening exercises.[2]

I would like to address myself to this topic by describing how an interdisciplinary team of three teachers in three traditional classrooms with 105 students of third through seventh year in school initiated the learning-center concept during the school year.

During the planning stages (previously discussed) they decided to use one classroom as the Mathematics Learning Center, one classroom for the Language Arts Learning Center, and the other classroom for the Social Studies and Science Learning Center. In each of these learning-center rooms the teachers planned to house all the materials, equipment, supplies, teaching aids, etc., appropriate for the discipline. For example, everything related to mathematics (manipulative materials, math filmstrips with projector, math textbooks, etc.) was housed in the Math Learning Center.

---

[2]*Ibid.,* pp. 21-22.

A modular schedule board was made for each of the learning centers. Each board listed the stations (by number) housed in the learning center and the time blocks for the day (see Figure 8-11).

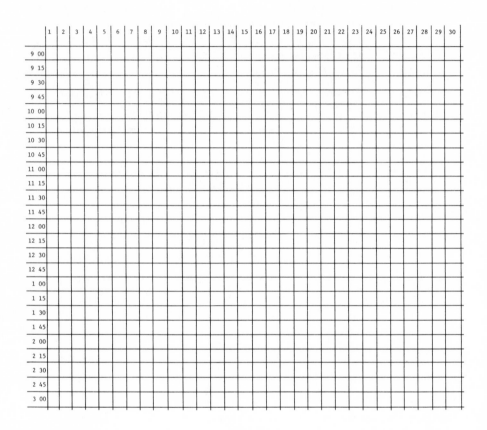

Figure 8-11

Initially, 60 learning stations (20 math, 20 language arts, 20 social studies and science) were made by the teachers. During a weekend the teachers rearranged one of the classrooms and set up these 60 stations in different areas of the room. On Monday morning all of the 105 children got a brief overview of how the learning centers and learning stations would work.

Teaching Students to Use Learning Stations

During the first week of operation one of the teachers explained to and worked with eight of the most self-directed students in the team. These students learned how to use the schedule board, work with the stations and to evaluate their work. During the next week, each of these eight students helped another student learn the process. The following week, these 16 students helped 16 more. This procedure continued until all the students had learned the process.

The teachers spent their planning time making more stations (180 in all) during the first three weeks of the training sessions by the students. After the third week, a weekend was spent in moving the stations to the appropriate learning center.

After the initial five-week period, all of the students had learned the process. All of the students did not work all of the stations. Some were prescribed by teachers as needed, and some were chosen by students because of interest.

Each teacher assumed the major responsibility for one of the learning centers. However, all of the teachers worked at times in all of the centers. Each had a homeroom group; however, all of the children were free to use all of the centers.

Student Self-Scheduling and Self-Evaluation

This conversion to the learning-station approach did not mean there was no direct teaching by the teachers. However, the emphasis was on learning rather than teaching. As the teachers moved around the centers and observed students working the stations, they recognized individuals with common needs and planned group instruction to satisfy these needs.

Each day, each student spent a 15-minute module for scheduling himself in each of the Centers by visiting each schedule board and placing his initials in a box on the board to reserve stations for specific mods for the next day. The student also recorded his schedule for an entire week. (See Figure 8-1 for a sample of a student's weekly schedule.)

At the end of each day, each student spent a few minutes writing notes about his accomplishments of the day. These notes (self-evaluation) were used by students when they had their weekly conferences with the teacher. These schedules and notes also became part of his permanent record. Samples of his work, chosen by himself and the teacher, were also included in his record.

Teacher-Pupil Conferences

Group and individual conferences are a must in the learning-center approach to teaching. An individual conference should be held at least bi-weekly with each student. For some students conferences should be more frequent.

During these times the student discusses with the teacher the stations he has accomplished and what he plans to do next. He evaluates his progress with the teacher and together they discuss any weaknesses or problems that either feels a need to consider. During these discussions the teacher prescribes those stations he feels the student needs to work on.

Record Keeping

The teacher keeps written records of conferences to add to the student's individual folder. Sample forms which could supplement a narrative record are included in Figures 8-12 and 8-13.

During conference time the teacher should clarify with the student the objectives of certain stations and guide the student to determine which stations to do when, which materials will be needed and why the stations should be done.

Name		Date:	From	To

Old Centers To Finish

Language Arts	Math	Science	Social Studies	Teacher/Student Comments

New Centers Prescribed

Language Arts	Math	Science	Social Studies	Teacher/Student Comments

Figure 8-12

Name _____ Date of Schedule _____

Module	Language Arts	Math	Social Studies	Science	Research (Media)	Scheduled PE, Art, Music
9:00						
9:15						
9:30						
9:45						
10:00						
10:15						
10:30						
10:45						
11:00						
11:15						
11:30						
11:45						
12:00						
12:15						
12:30						
12:45						
1:00						
1:15						
1:30						
1:45						
2:00						
2:15						
2:30						
2:45						
3:00						
3:15						

Teacher Comments:

Figure 8-13

ADVANTAGES OF THE LEARNING-CENTER APPROACH

The concept of learning centers is built on the premise that better learning opportunities can be made available for more individual students whose learning styles and rates are unique. Students function better in a less-restricted, presssure-free atmosphere. This open-classroom environment also frees the teacher to work with small groups and individuals while other students are involved in meaningful activities.

Perhaps the most important outcome of the learning-center approach is a change in attitude toward school. Rather than just being a place where one has to be from nine to three, school becomes an exciting part of living. Some specific advantages include:

- a relaxed and happy atmosphere with openness in pupil-teacher relationships;
- increased opportunities for flexible grouping to meet individual needs;
- children find more satisfaction in learning;
- children develop a sense of responsibility and greater self-discipline;
- the development of more positive "self" concepts;
- emphasis on learning rather than on teaching;
- creativity is enhanced;
- increased opportunities for diagnosis, prescription and evaluation of individual learning needs;
- less competition and more cooperation among students;
- more human interaction;
- classroom living based on real-life processes.

—SUMMARY—

The most important characteristic of team teaching and the learning-center approach is the "human" element. In this chapter it has been shown that through the utilization of learning centers a child can work independently with a series of related activities designed to promote understandings of certain concepts and how, ultimately, a child will develop the ability to schedule himself and discipline himself to carry out his own scheduled activities.

The main function of the instructional materials center is to help the teaching teams perform the educational process most effectively through making all kinds of books, instructional materials and equipment available for use in the other learning centers and at home as well as in the IMC.

Learning stations can be used by one teacher in a self-contained classroom as well as by teams of teachers. The use of learning centers and learning stations provides for all children the opportunity to grow in unique ways in an open-classroom atmosphere.

chapter nine | Facilities for Open Classrooms

Many educators are reluctant to encourage the development of open classrooms because they say the flexibility required in such a program is not possible in a traditional building. This is just an excuse, not a reason. Open classrooms can and have been housed in traditional facilities.

The open classroom embodies a philosophy that promotes flexible arrangements to permit individualized learning and continuous growth. Open classrooms are enhanced by modern school plants. However, a modern open-space building is not a prerequisite. The building is far less important than the human element.

We need to view students as persons who are enacting roles in a school situation; therefore, we need to provide the kind of educational program that brings the school's expectation of student roles and the students' own expectations into close harmony. We need to use the students' own values for continuing guidance in decision-making that will lead both pupils and teachers toward more meaningful approaches to relationships with each other. The emphasis should be upon learning by the pupils, with student self-control a number-one goal.

Most human learning is not the result of instruction, but rather the result of interrelationships of human beings in social situations. Creating open classrooms includes arranging school facilities, providing materials, managing social relationships and activities to promote worthwhile and productive living for children.

Each pupil needs to feel important; each needs to know that the purposes of the open classroom are to meet his needs and concerns, to help him overcome his fears and anxieties, and to satisfy his curiosities. Well-planned programs should include content, activities, and materials pertaining to human relationships in the home, school and community. Experiences should be provided to help children become effective as individuals and as group members.

Children need to become skillful in human relations, economically efficient and accepting of certain civic responsibilities. In order for these values to be really learned by children they must be lived in all phases of the school program.

Children must be taught to set purposes and to use their freedom wisely in achieving their goals and objectives. Freedom is the power of effective choice; choice demands viable alternatives. In the open classroom, freedom should be *for* instruction, not *from* instruction. This new freedom is toward self-direction and self-discipline. Emphasis must be upon what pupils actually do rather than on what is done for pupils.

Open classrooms are enhanced by the encouragement of diversity and creativity. Creativity means action. We need to provide an ever-increasing variety and number of activities that will give opportunities for individuals to express their ideas, imagination, and experiences. Motivation comes from the satisfaction of seeing one's ideas take on meaning.

All of these tenets of the open-classroom philosophy are possible in any type of physical structure. Many people use the terms "open classrooms" and "open-space school" synonomously. However, they do not mean the same thing. An open-space school is a facility—a place; an open classroom is a philosophy—a way of life.

Open classrooms are in operation in self-contained rooms in traditional buildings as well as in modern open-space schools. The open classroom is an environmental atmosphere with the spotlight on the learner and what he is "doing." On the other hand, one can find open-space schools where the teachers separate the instructional areas by using movable bookcases and cabinets as walls and, thus, create self-contained classrooms where Jack is in the box.

Innovations grow out of the involvement of teachers, principal, children, parents and the community in planning cooperatively and working together. By sharing ideas and responsibility, creativity is stimulated. If you have a conviction that the open-classroom concept is what is needed in your situation—traditional building or modern open-space school— then develop a commitment to the philosophy and approach the change with confidence.

chapter ten

Open Classrooms in an Open School in an Open Community

Creating open classrooms means providing adults and children with opportunities to develop personal relationships that nourish their growth. These relationships must be based upon mutual trust and communication.

Learning is an individual matter. Each child must become actively involved in the process in order for learning to occur. Educators must accept each student for whatever he is and for whatever he can do.

We can stimulate the learner's interests and help him develop self-confidence. We must care for him and give him freedom to think and feel and do. There are many aspects of the environment and the curriculum that can be planned to help students and adults relate well with each other.

This final chapter is a description of the environment and program of Longfellow Elementary School. Through this description it is hoped that the reader will see how the ideas presented in this book have been implemented. One should gain an understanding of the attitudes toward children and learning and the kind of relationships necessary in order to create open classrooms in an open school.

LONGFELLOW NEIGHBORHOOD IN COLUMBIA, MARYLAND

The planned community of Columbia was discussed at length in Chapter Five. It is a people-centered community. The community is the setting in which the child lives and learns, in which he develops meanings and concepts essential to an understanding of group living. In this setting he experiences life in a democrmxy. Experiences in church, stores, theatres, home, neighborhood and school become his background for study, thought, and expression.

The community is the child's laboratory for learning about man's way of living because it provides first-hand experiences in the social functions of group living. Some of the richest instructional resources are found in the local community. Children can cooperate in local projects and become participants in community activities. The child's own daily experiences in the community are a resource that can enrich learning in the open classroom.

The Columbia plan starts with a neighborhood of 800 to 1,200 families. Near the center of each neighborhood is an elementary school, park and playground, swimming pool, small community building and a convenience store. Longfellow is one such neighborhood.

Longfellow Elementary is an "interaction school." (See Chapter Five, Figure 5-1.) It is the center of community life. The school as well as the neighborhood is named for the American poet, Henry Wadsworth Longfellow. The names of the streets in the neighborhood are taken from his writings: Hesperus Drive, Even Star Place, Summer Day Lane, Iron Pen Place, etc.

Figure 10-1

Physical Facilities

In the introduction to *Hiawatha,* Longfellow tells of how the spirit *Manitou* called all the Indian tribes together to bury their weapons and smoke the peace pipe. Using the Indian motif, the students are divided into four tribes: Comanche, Mohawk, Omaha, and Pawnee. Part of the Pawnee "reservation" is set aside for the Tenderfeet (Kindergarten) of the Pawnee Tribe. (See Figure 10-2 for a diagram of this "Indian Village.")

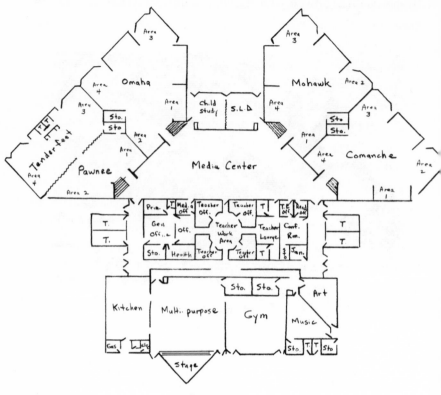

Figure 10-2

The "hunting grounds" include the vast media center, multi-purpose room, gym, music center, art center, outside area, including a small woods, and the entire neighborhood and community. These areas provide each Indian with numerous opportunities to explore and discover.

Philosophy of the School

The major goal of the program is to help each child find and develop his "way of life." The objectives are to help each: find satisfaction in learning; realize that subject matter skills are the tools he should use in meeting and solving his everyday problems; develop self-confidence; think imaginatively and openly explore his ideas; free himself to explore the resources of the school and community as well as his own resources; develop self-direction and self-discipline in order to assume responsibility for his own learning. Emphasis is placed upon learning (what pupils actually do) rather than upon instruction (what is done for pupils).

Each pupil has purposes of his own and a pattern of growth which he must follow in order to develop his feelings and his attitudes. An attempt has been made to arrange school facilities, provide materials, and manage social relationships and activities that will promote worthwhile and productive living for children. Evaluation is in terms of the quality of living of every child.

Team (Tribe) Organization

Each teaching team includes four teachers, one of which is designated as tribe "chief" (team leader). The Pawnee tribe includes the Kindergarten (Tenderfeet) and first, second, and third year students. In the Omaha tribe are students in first, second, third, and fourth year. Mohawks include second, third, fourth, and fifth year students. The Comanche tribe has third, fourth, and fifth year students.

Each team has total team planning time for one hour each on two days weekly, 30 minutes daily during the lunch period, and 30 minutes at the end of the school day. In addition, each has a 30-minute, duty-free lunch period. The reading specialist is assigned to each team daily for the language arts time. This provides an extra teacher for the reading period. She not only works with remedial cases, but with accelerated students as well; she has 90 minutes each day for individuals, small-group work, and evaluation. In this manner she is a resource teacher for the entire staff.

Each special teacher (vocal music, phys. ed., media, and art) is scheduled for one period per week with each receiving group. The rest of the week is unscheduled to permit individual and small-group work as needs are analyzed. The lunchroom is supervised by the principal (nicknamed "Superchief" by the little Indians) and parent volunteers. Students may pursue special interests during the lunch hour because the special teachers are available (playground or gym, media center, music room, etc.). Lunch time interest groups also include such things as Spanish Class. (See schedule of special teachers in Figure 10-3.)

Other available specialists include an instrumental music teacher, speech therapist, child study center teacher and aide, special learning disabilities teacher, and a visiting art team. In addition to these regularly assigned specialists, services are available from the central office staff of the Howard County Public Schools.

A very important part of the total school team includes the principal's secretary, the teachers' secretary, the custodial staff, the cafeteria personnel and the more than 100 volunteer aides.

Flexible Grouping and Instruction

Longfellow is a nongraded school. This requires flexibility in grouping. Groupings are based on the needs of children regardless of age or grade. The needs of each individual are different and constantly changing. Since nongrading is concerned with meeting individual needs, the groupings change as needs change.

Each receiving area (homeroom) is a heterogeneous group

Schedule of Special Teachers

Code: C=Comanche Tribe   M=Mohawk Tribe   O=Omaha Tribe   P=Pawnee Tribe

TIME	TUESDAY Media	TUESDAY Music	TUESDAY PE	TUESDAY Art	WEDNESDAY Music	WEDNESDAY PE	THURSDAY Media	THURSDAY Music	THURSDAY PE	THURSDAY Art
9:00	M #1	M #2	M #3	M #4	P #1	P #2	M #3	M #4	M #1	M #2
9:30	M #2	M #3	M #4	M #1	P #2	P #1	M #4	M #1	M #2	M #3
10:00	C #4	C #2	C #1	C #3			C #1	C #3	C #4	C #2
10:30	C #2	C #1	C #3	C #4			C #3	C #4	C #2	C #1
11:00										
11:30										
12:00										
12:30										
1:15	O #1	O #2	O #3	O #4			O #3	O #4	O #1	O #2
1:45	O #2	O #3	O #4	O #1			O #4	O #1	O #2	O #3
2:15							P #1			P #2
2:45							P #2			P #1

Figure 10-3

(different ages and different levels). This grouping is used for adminstrative matters, student advising, and instruction in art, music, media and physical education. Students are grouped and regrouped within each team on a multi-age achievement basis for instruction in the skill areas of language arts and mathematics. There is also some regrouping, based on achievement, between teams as individual needs change.

In order to provide opportunities for children to be with those of their own age for part of the day, science and social studies are taught to groups based on year in school. At a designated time during the day all fifth year students move to the multi-purpose room, all fourth year students go to the Comanche reservation, the third year students assemble in the Mohawk area, the seconds move to the Omaha reservation and the first year students meet in the Pawnee area.

Interest groupings are available during the lunch period as well as other times during the day (See Figure 10-4). There are also planned times for grouping by sex—all boys of a tribe have one activity while all the girls have another. Each Kindergarten section has use of the outside play area or the multi-purpose room for activities such as creative dance, rope climbing, large-group games. While one section utilizes this space the other section utilizes the entire Kindergarten area for a variety of learning acitivites, individual and small-group work (See Figure 10-5). At the midpoint of the session both groups come together for snacks and social activities. After snack time the groups trade spaces.

Instruction is planned to facilitate individualized learning. Individual needs are analyzed, learning activities prescribed, and evaluation is continuous. A variety of materials and activities is provided to meet individual needs. These activities include: meaningful learning stations (See Figure 10-6); large-group instruction (See Figure 10-7); teacher-directed lessons (See Figure 10-8); small-group projects (See Figure 10-9); independent study (See Figure 10-10); one-to-one situations (See Figure 10-11); discussions (with and without adult leadership) (See Figure 10-12); and free access to the media center (See Figure 10-13). The grouping is very flexible and is changed whenever a need arises.

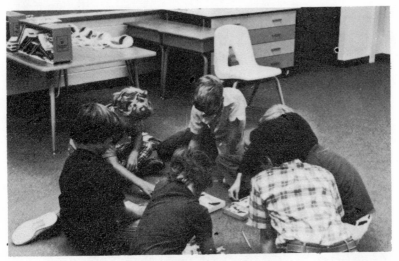

Figure 10-4

Figure 10-5

Figure 10-6

Figure 10-7

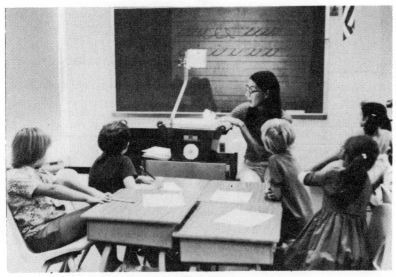

Figure 10-8

Figure 10-9

Figure 10-10

Figure 10-11

Figure 10-12

Figure 10-13

Children with Special Learning Disabilities[1]

Longfellow is one of the schools in Howard County that has the services of special education programs. There are two special education resource rooms housed in the school with a specially trained teacher assigned to each. In addition, an instructional aide is assigned to the Child Study room.

The children who need these special services are ones who have potential but, for a variety of reasons, have been unable to progress academically in the regular instructional program. The behavior of these children may vary from ones who appear to daydream to ones who are in constant motion and seemingly unable to attend to the assignment given. They are distracted by noises, movements of others, or by the items in the classroom. They may not remain at one task for a reasonable amount of time in order to complete it but rather jump from one activity to another with no real purpose. On the other hand, they may sit and repeat the same thing over and over again when it is not necessary. Some tend to be irritable, aggressive and destructive. They may be unable to control their emotions and act in ways that are inappropriate at given times. Because of past failures in schoolwork, they may not like school.

Some children, although they do not suffer any *physical* hearing loss, do have difficulty in understanding what they hear. Thus, they do not respond to directions correctly or interpret oral language properly. In addition, they may have problems in expressing themselves. Some of these children have great difficulty in remembering. This may show up in regard to remembering past experiences, lessons supposedly learned or things to be done.

---

[1]Taken from Child Study Center, Special Education, Procedure Manual 1972, Howard County Public Schools, Clarksville, Maryland. Used by permission.

Physically, these children may show signs of awkwardness. They are often so poorly coordinated that they cannot catch or bounce a ball, jump, hop or skip. Not only do they have difficulties in controlling large-muscle activities, but their small-muscle development also lags.

The Child Study Program operates an interdisciplinary diagnostic service for any pupil who is referred to it. Such referrals are accepted at any time during the school year and such children are evaluated in depth by the nurse, pediatrician, psychologist, speech and hearing clinician, and special education teachers, as needs indicate. A major focus of the program is to identify learning disabilities early in the school experience and to set up remedial programs of instruction to correct the problems and to offset the results of accumulated failure among bright children. Those children so identified receive special help for a minimum of 45 minutes per day in one of the resource rooms.

The goal of the program is to keep children with specific learning disabilities in the mainstream of educational pursuits without transporting them away from their home schools or assigning them to full-time, self-contained special education classes.

Student Involvement

In the introduction to *Hiawatha*, Manitou called together several Indians from each of the tribes to form a council. Longfellow School has such a council composed of four representatives from each tribe and the four officers elected by the students to lead their student council.

One of the activities organized and operated by the council is the school newspaper, *Smoke Signals*. The students write the

AS THE NEWLY ELECTED HEAD OF THE STUDENT COUNCIL
I WANT TO MAKE ONE THING CRYSTAL CLEAR.....
I AM THE PRESIDENT!

articles, type, set up the "dummy," help the secretary duplicate the paper, and handle the circulation. The council meets regularly to consider concerns, suggestions, and ideas presented to them by members of the various tribes. One such concern is that of keeping the school attractive by displaying arts and crafts throughout the building. The familiar "peace sign" with the hand also means "friend" in Indian language. This has become an outward and visible sign of their concern about caring for each other and promoting peace and harmony throughout this "Indian Village."

Volunteers

There are more than 100 volunteer aides assisting at the school. In addition to parent and community aides, there are student aides from the local high school. Some of the duties of the volunteers are: taking attendance; keeping routine records; collecting funds for various purposes; working in the health room; correcting objective tests and making up lists and charts for teachers; helping supervise playground and lunchroom activities; assisting in the media center; caring for and operating audio-visual equipment; typing and duplicating; answering the telephone; filing work in children's folders; making arrangements for field trips; assisting children in construction of bulletin boards; and listening to and sharing thoughts with children.

One volunteer serves as coordinator of all the other volunteers. She helps see that the teachers get the kinds of help they need and also that volunteers are assigned to the kinds of tasks they prefer.

In open classrooms, where each child is being instructed on his own achievement level, teacher aides and volunteers help teachers individualize instruction and fulfill the goals established for the program. The more adults sharing the workload the more successful the program can be in meeting the unique needs of individuals.

By using these volunteers, the school is able to free the teachers of many time-consuming tasks and clerical jobs, and thus, to provide them with more opportunities for individualizing instruction.

Teacher-Education Center

Longfellow Elementary is involved in a partnership with the University of Maryland, Baltimore County (UMBC). A Teacher-Education Center Coordinator and a secretary have been jointly appointed and financed by the school system and UMBC. The coordinator develops and operates an in-service program for teachers and plans the pre-service activities for student teachers, field experience students, and students from on-campus courses.

Although prospective teachers can be taught in groups, they learn as individuals; they learn at different rates, with different styles, and in response to different stimuli. An individualized instructional plan is designed to provide learning materials of varying levels of difficulty presented in a variety of ways. The role of the coordinator in an individualized program is to diagnose the learning and personal characteristics of each prospective teacher and to select appropriate educational activities to meet specific behavioral objectives.

The setting in which teacher education occurs cannot be separated from the instructional program. The open classrooms at Longfellow are designed to be neutral so that they can be molded by the users to meet their own unique needs. Open classrooms encourage movement, exploration, discovery, inter-action and cooperation among and between pre-service and in-service teachers. The development of human relations skills is a major concern.

Performance objectives are utilized as the basis of the program to permit prospective teachers to demonstrate compe-tency in teaching prior to certification. Flexibility is built into the training sequences so that there are alternative methods of realizing objectives.

A variety of field experiences is provided early in the program and continued throughout the training period to permit trainees to try out their style of teaching. Teacher preparation is viewed as a continuous, lifelong process, rather than one ending with graduation.

The School is the "Heart" of the Neighborhood

The Longfellow Elementary School is open evenings and weekends for a variety of activities such as boy scouts, brownies, karate, fencing, discussion groups, table games, and sports. This program was initiated with an every-home visit by concerned persons. Following are information sheets and survey forms that were personally distributed and discussed.

DO YOUR THING

THE NEW LONGFELLOW COMMUNITY SCHOOL

INVITES YOU TO BE A...

GIVER

TAKER

PARTICIPATOR

DROP IN FREE PROGRAMS ALL AGES

LET'S ALL GET TOGETHER AND DO OUR THING!

THE PROGRAM IS YOU.

Dear Neighbors,

In a community school the traditional role of the neighborhood school is expanded from that of a formal learning center for the young, operating 6 hours a day, 5 days a week, 39 weeks a year. . . .to a total community Opportunity Center for young and old, operating after classes into the night, Saturdays, school vacations, and summertime.

The community school is many things to many people. To some it is adult education and enrichment courses. To others it is recreation and new faces. The community school can be many things to many people, for people-determine scope and nature of the community.

Many people in the neighborhood of Longfellow have already expressed needs and desires that could be met by a community school operation. Many more people have not expressed their needs. The community school is a vehicle that can allow for expression of these needs as well as provide an instrument to help meet some of those needs.

Community education is a concept more than a thing which serves the entire community by providing for the needs of the community. It uses the local school and other agencies to serve as a catalyst to bring community resources to bear on community problems.

However, the community school has more to offer than problem-orientated projects. It can enrich an entire community by enriching the members of that community. To the proponents of community education, it is the utilization of facilities, people, and resources in the furtherance of the education of everyone in the community.

In establishing and maintaining a community school there are several problems of organization and many questions to be answered. The most common structure is the Neighborhood Council. The Neighborhood Council is made up of volunteers from the community who accept the responsibility of organizing and administering the community school. Their responsibility includes: 1) encouraging informed citizen participation; 2) fact-finding; 3) developing public understanding and support; 4) coordinating community activities and services; and 5) reflecting the needs and desires of the community.

Schools make excellent community centers because they are located so as to serve neighborhoods. They have facilities adaptable to broad community uses. They are owned and supported by the public. They are there.

Let's Open Our Schools for All People of All Ages at All Times for Fun, Learning, Growth and Recreation.

Arts and Crafts

block printing, lettering, drawing, holiday decorations, centerpieces, copper enameling, antiquing, macramé, crocheting, embroidery, knitting, quilting, decoupage, collage, gift wrapping, paper craft, lapidary, rock polishing, sculpture, leather craft, candle making, needle point, painting, water color, oil, tole, china, pottery, ceramics, mosaics, rugs, hooked, braided, weaving, caning, wigs and vogues, hat making, wood working, taxidermy, electric etching.

Musical/Theatrical Activities

band, orchestra, choral groups, sing-alongs, shows, fashion, pet, variety, magicians, folk festival, music appreciation, banjo, guitar, piano instruction, instrumental group, theatre, adult, children, community.

Food Preparation
Household Management

baking, cake decorating, balanced diets, meal planning, candy making, cooking, inexpensive casseroles, foreign baking, preparing wild game, party foods.

Recreation

archery, basketball, shuffleboard, volleyball, badminton, horseshoes, ping-pong, handball, wrestling, tennis, golf, card playing (and tournaments), pinochle, bridge, cribbage, chess, checkers, modern, social, square, tap, folk, ballet and teen dances, family movies, technical films, bingo, travel films, fishing skills, fly typing, gymnastics, tumbling, physical fitness class, recreation, skating, ice and roller skating, slow pitch softball adult (drop-in), football adults (drop-in), track and field events, turtle races, TV sports viewing, football, basketball, yoga, judo, karate, weight lifting.

Special Activities

After school supervised activities, area beautification, service to the community, art for pre-school child and parent, pre-school story hour, contemporary problems, field trips, skiing, sports events, harbor tours, job discussion with younger people, lecture series, inter-personal relationships, parent/child relationships, how to be a parent, delinquency problems, self-understanding, teens and tensions, the one-parent family, mental health services (confidential), senior citizens activities, (day, night), study area for students, trading post, magazines, sports equipment, musical instruments, astronomy, auto repair, tuneup, appliance repair, child care for baby sitters, charm classes, clothing alterations and design, citizenship education, parliamentary procedure, introduction to computers, English for foreign born, first aid, home nursing, expectant parents class, foreign language (French, German, Spanish), furniture repair, refinishing, upholstering, grooming, home repairs, remodeling, carpentry, improvement of study skills, interior decoration, reweaving, landscaping, tree pruning, gardening, mechanical drawing, reading blue prints, pet care, obedience class, planning family finances, consumer protection class, principles of insurance, real estate, radio and TV troubleshooting, photography, reading and writing improvements, shorthand, securities and investments, civil service tests, income tax preparation, speed reading, public speaking, typing, stretch and sew, Bishop sewing, dress making, tailoring, what's new in the school room, modern math for parents, how to plan a vacation.

CLUBS—groups with similar interests
(Your skill is not important)

Actors, drama, artists, painters, puppetry clowns, amateur radio, electronics, science, barber shop quartet, sweet adelines, baton twirling, bicycling, rocketry, Big Brothers, Big Sisters, book discussion, film discussion, job discussion, investments, car-pool, genealogy, canoeing, canoe-building, racing, scuba diving, skiing, collectors—coins, stamps, rocks, insects, leaves, fisherman, hunters, boaters, birdwatchers, go-cart building and racing, hobby, journalists, creative writing, Jr. achievement, model making of cars, boats, planes, take-off pounds, stop smoking, jogging, gymnasts, toastmasters, toastmistresses, parents, singles, Jr. teens, Sr. teens, card playing, pinochle, cribbage, bridge, cooking, sewing, homemakers, dancing—folk, square, social and many, many others.

OTHERS

_____

_____

_____

_____

_____

LEISURE TIME SURVEY

Your name_____ Phone number_____

Address_____

This survey is an invitation to every person in the area to express interests and to share with us your feeling about using YOUR SCHOOLS in the evenings and weekends. Simply list at the bottom of this page any activity in which you or other members of your household feel you would like to participate . . . if it were offered at our school.

1. Are there any leisure time activities in which you or others of your household are presently engaged outside your neighborhood that you would prefer to do closer to your home?_____

Place of Facility	Activity or program
_____	_____
_____	_____
_____	_____

2. List any unmet recreational, educational, social, civic or other need which "bugs" you or any other member of your household.

_____

_____

3. Do you know of any organization or group that might be interested in using the schools evenings or on weekends? (specify)___

4. Would you be interested in any of the following?

(a) Serving on neighborhood council?_____

(b) Assisting with supervision evenings or weekends?_____

(c) Donating materials or equipment?_____(specify)___

_____

(d) Other? _____(specify)_____

5. If you have a skill or interest in any activity and would be willing to volunteer your services as an instructor, please indicate the subject(s). Would you instruct/tutor/lead?_____

6. Please indicate below those activities in which you or other household members are genuinely interested and would partici-pate. . . .if offered. (Such as Educational Enrichment courses, Arts and Crafts, Recreation, Musical/Theatrical, Food Preparation/House-hold Management, etc.) Be specific, for example, watercolor painting, guitar instruction, consumer protection class, etc.

_____	_____
_____	_____
_____	_____
_____	_____
_____	_____
_____	_____

Please use the space below for suggestions or additional comments.

This survey is sponsored by the Longfellow Elementary School, Longfellow Elementary P.T.A. and the Recreation Committee of the Harper's Choice Village Board plus many, many individual neighbors in Longfellow.

LONGFELLOW COMMUNITY SCHOOL
FIRST COURSE OFFERINGS

Based on interest, questionnaire results and the help of many people we are beginning the following courses:

MONDAY

Children's Theatre — 7:00 p.m. starting November 6 — Bonnie Schiff 997-2184.
Cross Country Skiing — 8:00 p.m. preparation meeting, November 13 Linda Gottfield — 730-1464.
Beginning Sewing — 7:30 p.m. October 23, Amelia Rogers — 730-6545.
Stretch & Sew — 7:30 November 1, Mary Schuhle — 730-1691.
Water Colors — 7:30 p.m. October 23 — Carolyn Latanision — 730-8158.

TUESDAY

Chess Playing and Learning Club — 7:00 p.m. October 24, Bill Lagley — 730-8352
Choral Group — 8:00 p.m. Tuesday nights, already begun — Duane Smith — 730-4275
Decoupage — 7:30 p.m. November 14 — Ilene Zeitzer — 730-0176
Exercise Class — 8:00 p.m. Tuesday nights, already begun — Michelle Laudadio — 730-0847

WEDNESDAY

Bicycle Maintenance — 7:00 p.m. October 25 — Gene Fremanis — 730-5169
House Wiring — 8:00 p.m. November 1 — Michael Deutsch — 730-6944
Sailboat Handling — 7:00 November 1 — Leslie Gordon — 997-1884
Modern Dance for Children — 4:00 Oct. 24 Laura Deutsch — 730-6944

THURSDAY

Bridge Learning and Playing — 8:00 p.m. October 26 — Jo Fitz-gibbons — 730-0890

Consumer Protection — 7:00 p.m. October 26 — Vic Ganderson
            997-1946
Genealogy — 8:00 p.m. October 26 — Sheila Scott — 997-1064
Oil Painting — 7:30 p.m. October 26 — Roberta Martin — 997-2542

FRIDAY

Card Playing — 7:30 p.m. November 10 — John Murphy — 730-0107
Children's Art — 7:00 p.m. October 27 — Karen Schuster —
            997-1163
Tennis —6:00 p.m. November 1 — Carol Langley — 730-8352
Travel Log Film/Slides Series — 8:00 p.m. November 10 — Doug
            Bivens — 730-3373
Sailboat Making — Date and time unknown — call Gerald Dance —
            997-2159
Furniture Making — Date and time unknown — Call above.
Modern Dance for Adults — if interested call Laura Deutsch —
            730-6944

All activities will be held in the Longfellow Elementary School.

Since your neighbors will be sharing their knowledge with you, all
activities are free.

For further information call: Curt Miles   730-4096
                                 Deborah Polin   730-1296

A volunteer coordinator makes all necessary arrangements for scheduling, proper supervision, and clean-up for all activities. The coordinator is a work-study student, made available through the Howard County Teachers Association.

The Columbia Association sponsors an after-school neighborhood recreation program at the school three days a week—one day is for arts and crafts, one for sports, and one for special events. This program is free to all children of the neighborhood.

A Day Care Program is offered to children of working parents. It is an integral part of the total development of children with planned educational activities before school as well as after school. These activities are organized and supervised by qualified personnel.

Through community involvement the school has become the center of community life. The school is a place where the learning process is continually evolving. Longfellow Elementary is a breathing part of the everyday experience of each member of the neighborhood. This is the philosophy of the open classroom.

OPEN EDUCATION – SUMMARY

O–OPEN EDUCATION is a philosophy of education based upon a humanistic approach to teaching in order to meet the differing social, mental, and physical needs of each student. It supports organizational plans that eliminate grade labels, promote flexible grouping and continuous progress, and permit the utilization of meaningful individualized instruction.

P–PLANNING requires a team approach. We need a cooperative effort of the professionals, paraprofessionals, support personnel (clerical, cafeteria, custodial), parents, children, and the community. All must be involved in planning the program.

E–ENTHUSIASM–We must make a commitment to the philosophy of open education and enthusiastically accept the responsibility of creating an atmosphere that will free each person so that he may contribute to the process of becoming.

N–NEW FREEDOM–Freedom is the power of effective choice; choice demands viable alternatives. Freedom is a mental attitude; it is not an end in itself, but a means by which thinking, judging, evaluating, and acting may be integrated into the development of individual capacity. In open classrooms, freedom should be for instruction, not from instruction. This new freedom is toward self-direction and self-discipline. Emphasis must be upon learning (what pupils actually do) rather than on instruction (what is done for pupils).

E—ENVIRONMENT—We must create a relaxed atmosphere that will free each person from unnecessary pressure and allow him to develop his creative potential. School must be a "fun" place—not a place where you go to experience pain for five or six hours a day and then go elsewhere to experience pleasure. School should be a continuation of one's style of living. Learning must be kept alive, for children learn as they live. The school should be the center of community life.

D—DIVERSITY—The philosophy of the open classroom is enhanced by the encouragement of diversity and creativity. Through this encouragement, the individual has a chance to be himself without coercion from others. A diversity of groups and activities gives him the opportunity to find himself at ease in the groups that satisfy his needs.

U—UNDERSTANDING—Children look to teachers for guidance in the solution of their everyday problems; they expect teachers to be able to understand and help solve the problems of group living. They look to the teacher as an example. They see how she lives more than they hear what she tells them. Caring must be the teacher's "style of living."

C—CONCEPT OF SELF—A well-developed human being is one who has self-respect, because this is a basic need of all humans. A major task of the teacher is to help each child develop and maintain self-respect. Each needs a positive self-concept.

A—ATTITUDES AND VALUES—Children look to the teacher as the "expert" in human relations. Children should be guided in making decisions that will result in higher qualities of living. Teachers should help children interpret the values and attitudes that are developed through "living" together at school.

T—TEACHING—Instruction should be based upon diagnosis of individual needs. There should be continuous evaluation of each so that his needs may be analyzed, learning activities may be prescribed, and the proper materials may be provided to help him develop to his fullest potential. Teachers must provide learning activities that are relevant to the child; it is his right to understand the reason for each activity. When he needs the activity and sees how it is relevant to his way of life, then it will become meaningful for him, and then only will he "learn."

I—INDIVIDUALIZATION—We must be sincerely concerned about the welfare of each child and accept him for what he is. We can provide flexible grouping, one-to-one situations, or independent study and call this individualized instruction; but what we should really be concerned about is individualized learning. Regardless of the teaching alternatives we provide, the learning that takes place is by each individual. Each is a unique human being with purposes of his own and a pattern of growth that he must follow in order to develop *his* feelings and *his* attitudes because *his* living demands this.

O—OBJECTIVES of open education should be to help each child find and develop his "way of life." We should help each: find satisfaction in learning; realize that subject matter skills are the tools he should use in meeting and solving his everyday problems; develop self-confidence; think imaginatively and openly explore his ideas; free himself to explore the resources of the school and community as well as his own resources; and develop self-direction and self-discipline in order to assume responsibility for his own learning.

N—NEEDS—Each individual needs physical activity; he needs to talk; he needs to be part of a small group; he needs time to work alone; he needs creative activities; he needs some large-group experiences; he needs to be himself. Most human learning is not the result of instruction, but rather the result of inter-relationships of human beings as they develop in social situations. We must arrange school facilities, provide materials, manage social relationships and activities that will promote worthwhile and productive living for children. We must evaluate our efforts in terms of the quality of living of every child.

—CONCLUSION—

Creating open classrooms means opening up the school lives of boys and girls to the wonderful world of knowledge. We must help each to see himself as a worthwhile human being able to make a contribution to the society in which he lives.

Those of us who witness this kind of growth and understanding in children realize that living and teaching in ʼopen classrooms is the only practical way to get JACK OUT OF THE BOX.

Index

A

Absentees, 112
Acceptance, 31
Accounts, 110
Achievement levels, 111
Achievement, scholastic, 40
Administrator:
  brainstorming meetings, 67
  community, 70-71
  conduct, 56
  continuous professional education, 57
  cooperative approach, 56
  creates relaxed atmosphere, 55
  demonstration lessons, 67-68
  desirable innovations, 57
  displays, 68
  "group-centered" discussions, 67
  group process, 63-64
  human relationships, 58
  independent study, 68
  individual differences within staff, 60
  in-service activities, 66-68
  in-service programs, 59-61
  instructional leader, 57
  interaction within school, 56
  interpersonal relationships, 71-72
  leadership behavior, 58
  leadership of ideas and values, 59
  leading group discussions, 56
  meaningful learning, 55
  mental health of teachers, 60
  morale, 56, 68-69
  needs of school and community, 59
  new information utilized, 59
  openness with faculty, 59
  principal-teacher relationship, 58
  problems essential to producing
    change, 59
  professional library, 68
  relating theory and practice, 60
  role in initiating change, 56
  sample bulletins for teachers, 61-66
  school board, 69
  security for children, 65-66
  self-direction and self-discipline,
    61-62
  seminars, 67
  sensitivity, 56
  sensitivity through role playing, 64-65
  sharing sessions, 67
  should program his learning, 61
  summary, 73-75
  supervisory responsibilities, 57-59
  time, 60
  "tone" of school, 55
  utilizing peer teachers, 62-63
  working with others, 56
  workshops, 66-67
Affect, 94-96
Age, 36-37, 39
Aggressiveness, 32, 216
Aides, 110-115
Appropriate Placement School, The, 37
Art, 141, 146, 165-166, 223
Attendance, 110
Attitudes, 21, 26, 29, 34
Audio-visual equipment, 110
Awkwardness, 217

B

"Bad behavior," 33
Back assignments, 112
Behavior, 40
Boswell, John G., 78

I

Imagination, 26
Inappropriate behavior, 216
Independence, 21, 26
Independent study, 144, 145
Individual differences, 20-21, 39-40
Individualized instruction, 39, 163
Individualized learning, 27-30
Individualized schedules, 180-182
Infant, 44
In-service activities, 66-68
In-service programs:
    individual differences within staff, 60
    mental health of teachers, 60
    new information utilized, 59
    problems essential to producing change, 59
    relating theory and practice, 60
    time, 60
Instructional Materials Center, 177-180
Instrumental music, 142, 146, 167
Interaction, 35, 220
Interdisciplinary team, 145
Interdisciplinary team teaching, 144
Interests, 40
Intermurals, 147
Interpersonal relationships, 27, 71-72
Involvement, student, 217-218
Irritability, 216

K

Karate, 220

L

Language arts, 140, 145
Large-muscle activities, 217
Lavatory periods, 110
Learning:
    aim of reading instruction, 45
    assuming responsibility for program

of instruction, 82
    change in behavior, 82
    concrete experiences, 45
    continuous, 44-46, 82
    continuous analysis, 45
    differences among individuals, 82
    difficulties, 145
    direct experiences, 45
    disabilities, 216-217
    discovery of one's potency, 82
    evidenced, 82
    freedom of choice, 82
    individual growth, 82
    individual matter, 82
    individualized, 27-30
    infant, 44
    initiating action, 82
    learning to learn, 91-94
    needs differ, 39
    personal involvement, 82
    process, not product, 44
    rates and styles, 38
    reacting to stimuli, 82
    reading activities, 45
    relationships drawn from experiences, 82
    stations, 182-184, 185-189, 190
    vocabulary and speech, 44-45
Learning center:
    actual geographical location, 175
    administrative matters, 175
    advantages, 196
    aim at individuality, 174
    assistance of teachers, 175
    characteristic behaviors of teacher, 173
    child works independently, 175
    child's schedule unique, 175
    classes scheduling, 175
    enlarged learning environment, 173
    establishing, 174
    evaluating, time, 175
    feedback system, 173
    freedom of movement, 176
    greater independence for learner, 173
    guiding pupils, 176
    homeroom organization, 175

M

V

W

DATE DUE

MAR 27 '79		
MAR 30 '79	APR 8 '8	APR 19 '82
APR 17 '79	APR 10	APR 2 '84
APR 15 '8		
AP 7 '82		
AP 26 '82		
AP 9 '84		

GAYLORD   PRINTED IN U.S.